A GOOD DEATH

D. GREGORY WARK

TABLE OF CONTENTS

FOREWORD

Two thousand years ago, in a small fishing village on the northern shore of the Sea of Galilee, four men demonstrated rare but genuine friendship by going beyond the call of duty to help a man who could not help himself.

Here's the story as it is recorded in the Bible in Mark 2 and Luke 5. A little-known Jewish teacher named Jesus was just getting started in His work of preaching, healing, feeding the hungry, and dying for the sins of humanity. His reputation as a radical but life-giving teacher was spreading as fast as His reputation as a miracle worker.

Even before Jesus and His small team of less-than-impressive disciples arrived at the Sea of Galilee, rumors of lepers being cleansed, demoniacs being delivered, and various diseases being healed were already saturating the area. The residents of Capernaum were about to find out that the rumors of Jesus having supernatural power were actually true. Watching a previously paralyzed man walk tends to remove all doubts about the reality of miracles.

The Bible does not tell us the name of the paralyzed man or the name of his four friends, but in a town as small as first century Capernaum, everyone either knew him personally or at least knew of his condition. What we do know about him is that he was paralyzed, and then he was not.

The unnamed paralyzed man would never have been able to get to Jesus and get his miracle without the help of four friends who put him on a stretcher, fought through the crowd, broke a hole in the roof, and lowered him into the over-crowded house where they interrupted the sermon Jesus was preaching. As always, Jesus was more than accommodating, pausing His sermon to respond with compassion to genuine faith.

After this odd face-to-face encounter with Jesus, the man who came through the roof left through the door. He arrived paralyzed both physically and spiritually. He left healed and forgiven. He arrived at the house carried on a stretcher. He went home carrying a stretcher. That's what happens when people meet Jesus.

A few months ago, I was flying back to Nashville, Tennessee from Cape Town, South Africa where I was one of 5,000 delegates from 58 nations at the Every Nation 2016 World Conference. On that long flight, I read an advanced copy of *A Good Death* and couldn't help but think about an unforgettable sermon by a Kenyan pastor that I heard at the conference. Page after page of *A Good Death* reminded me of Oscar Murui's message about the unnamed paralyzed man and his four friends.

After narrating the story from Mark 2, Oscar concluded with a challenge for every delegate to be "stretcher-bearers" for people who cannot get to Jesus without human help. He also challenged us to identify four friends who would be our "stretcher-bearers" when we need them most. He told us to write the names of four people who would get us to Jesus no matter what, who would be there for us during the darkest times, who would be willing to tear the roof off a house for us. We all need a few friends who will do whatever it takes to help us when we are too broken to help ourselves.

Sitting in that crowded plane, as I read *A Good Death* and pondered Oscar's message, I paused to pray a prayer of thanks for my long-time friend, Greg Wark, who has been a stretcher-bearer for many and no doubt would be one for me if the need should arise. We all need friends like Greg, who will tear a hole in the roof with his bare hands if that is what is needed. We also need to be that kind of friend to others.

Enough about Greg; now let me talk about this book. In a day when politically correct gender confusion is the norm, reading a book that unapologetically defends and clearly defines manhood is as refreshing as it is rare. While *A Good Death* is not specifically about manhood and was not exclusively written for men, nevertheless it fills a deep void of books for men. Men, women, boys, and girls desperately need biblical clarity about manhood, and *A Good Death* provides it.

If you are a man, I encourage you to read this book together with your "band of brothers" or your "stretcher-bearers." If you are a woman, I encourage you to read this book with your husband, boyfriend, or fiancé. I pray that God will use *A Good Death* to strike a deathblow to gender confusion and spark a revival of biblical manhood around the world.

Steve Murrell

President

Every Nation Churches and Ministries

DEDICATION

This book is dedicated to all the men and women of God who fought the good fight of faith to the finish. They each found a good death and are known as the "cloud of witnesses." Most of their names are not even mentioned and their memory has long since been forgotten but their glory is found in heaven. May we be worthy to carry on their great legacy!

"I will not be afraid of my enemies, but I will remember the Lord, great and awesome, and will fight for my brothers, my sons, my daughters, my wife, and my house."

Nehemiah 4:14

PREFACE

*"Cowards die many times before their deaths; the valiant
never taste of death but once."*

William Shakespeare

There is no more beautiful place in the world to me than the
Sierra Nevada Mountains stretching from Northern California
into Nevada. Every year since I was a young child my mother
and father would mandate trips there for our entire family. It was
the place where I found out who I was as a young man, where a
city boy was taught what life was "really like." We would
backpack into the deep wilderness and face the wild along with
our father who never seemed more happy than when he was
there with us. During those times we would see our father in his
element, one he encouraged us to embrace. Setting up the tent,
hauling and chopping the wood for the campfire, etc., those are
some of the fondest days in my remembrance.

Every single good memory I have of my family before we
were scattered by the early deaths of both our parents was
formed either in those mountains or in stories we told about
them. After I finished college and came to accept God's call on my
life I knew of no better place to go to make my stand for God.
Instinctively, I knew that a solemn moment outside the eyes of

men needed to happen before I entered the fight for the souls of men. I needed a mountaintop experience alone with God before I began my race. So I drove to the mountains with about six gallons of water and a bag of peanuts and spent several days there in prayer and fasting. Within a couple of days I was ready to make my oath to God. So I climbed to the top of the highest peak, looking down on one of God's most magnificent creations: "God, I will never quit You."

That was more than 30 years ago and I often go back to that day in my mind to relive it. Now looking back, I can say without any hesitation that if I were to do it all over again I would not have uttered the same oath. In retrospect, I consider my declaration hugely arrogant, especially considering the cloud of witnesses that were surely listening, not to mention the Holy Godhead. They know how many have taken such an oath in history only to throw in the towel soon after. They are aware that the list of those spoken of in the book of Hebrews, those whom I call the Bible Special Forces, is short too many names of those who started with all the right stuff but dropped out before the war was won.

I was standing on that mountain like most young guys, green and full of himself, knowing everything about the theory of ministry and nothing of the experience of ministry, declaring to God, "I will never quit You." Thinking back, I should have said, "God, I cannot do anything without You doing it through me. If You don't go before me I'm dust for sure!" The fact that I am still in the game today is not a testimony to my oath on that mountain but to God's commitment to love us no matter what.

One of the great gifts God gives to man is the promise of new beginnings. Second Corinthians 3:18 (KJV) says, "But we all, with open face beholding as in a glass the glory of the Lord, are changed into the same image from glory to glory, even as by the Spirit of the Lord." Beginning with salvation, we are given the hope that if we rightly live out one level of life we will graduate to another. And with each new level a new faith is required along with a greater commitment to the processes of God. There is something dramatic and life altering that happens to every Christian man when moving from one level of glory to another.

We become more vulnerable in this moment than in any time in life's journey. Like the children of Israel crossing over the river Jordan we have visions both of the past and the future available to us. The pressure is immense to choose whether to stay where we are and where we have become accustomed or take that great step into the future with unforeseen challenges. What happens in this moment will undoubtedly frame our legacy into perpetuity.

How people remember us, how we are spoken of by our sons and daughters, our spiritual sons and daughters, and those we have spent our lives attempting to positively impact will be determined by how we navigate this moment of transition. And let me make something very clear: success isn't possible if you are not prepared right. You can't just do this on the fly! Failure to prepare is in fact preparation for failure. It is my sincere hope that this book will give both those at the beginning of the race and those fighting somewhere in between the perspective needed to make it to the end successfully. God did not enlist us in this fight without all the tools necessary to finish it well. You can do this my friend; I know you can.

"Do justice to the weak and fatherless; maintain the rights of the poor and needy. Rescue them out of the hand of the wicked." Psalms 82:3-4

INTRODUCTION

"It is not death that a man should fear, but he should fear never beginning to live."

Marcus Aurelius

"And at three in the afternoon Jesus cried out in a loud voice, 'Eloi, Eloi, lema sabachthani?' (which means 'My God, my God, why have you forsaken me?')." **Mark 15:34 (NIV)**

This cry was not one of a defeated man succumbing to the wounds of his torturers. It was also not the acknowledgment of a life of failure and defeat. That cry was the declaration of the beginning of a good death. Jesus was declaring to creation, "I have finished my mission, completed what I was sent to accomplish, and emptied myself so that I may die to see another day."

Have you ever felt as if your soul was bleeding? You know that eerie sense that life is seeping from your innermost self. My soul has often bled for those who began the race of faith well, only to drop out near the end. The life of a Christian should not be lived out this way! In our day, it is a common occurrence for the people of God to quit before the finish. Each time I hear another tragic story of a man surrendering the holy calling of God for the curse of this world I can't help but ask, what has happened so that capitulation to the enemy of our souls became an option? How does something, never considered before, become an acceptable choice? Why is the road of godly vision paved with the guilty souls of those who didn't finish well? Why do countless numbers of Christians throw in the towel with the finish in sight? Why do moral breakdowns and scandals happen later in life? What causes a man of God to accept the idols he spent most of his life defeating?

It doesn't matter how great a leader you are, or how wonderful people think you are— you will face challenges that tempt you to forfeit your God-ordained purpose in life. You will be enticed to throw it all away, for something promising to fill the void in your heart. You need to be prepared for these seasons of weakness. Be battle ready, forever vigilant, with your arsenal full. Be fortified by surrounding yourself with the right people. Furthermore, you need to have the humility to admit your vulnerability. We must understand all of the requirements that come along with the call of God. The Christian life is a succession of battles, fought on varying fronts, throughout our lifetime. The Christian life is a life of war.

From beginning to end that fact will not change. Those who proclaim bliss and nothing but peace in the Christian experience are liars. They carry a message of deceit. "Beware lest anyone cheat you through philosophy and empty deceit, according to the tradition of men, according to the basic principles of the world, and not according to Christ" (Colossians 2:8 NKJV). Anyone can start the race! It is the finish that matters! The glory is in the finish!

W. Tozer wrote: —a book now well worn. I still turn often to the petitions I recorded in that book. I remind God often of what my prayers have been. One prayer in the book—and God knows it well by this time, for I pray it often—goes like this: 'Oh God, let me die rather than to go on day by day living wrong. I do not want to become a careless, fleshly old man. I want to be right so that I can die right. Lord, I do not want my life to be extended if it would mean that I should cease to live right and fail in my mission to glorify You all of my days! As you will recall from Second Kings 20, the Lord gave Hezekiah a 15-year extension of life. Restored to health and vigor, Hezekiah disgraced himself and dishonored God before he died and was buried. I would not want an extra 15 years in which to backslide and dishonor my Lord. I would rather go home right now than to live on—if living on was to be a waste of God's time and my own! Please, Father, help me to finish well. Amen.'"

"Finish the race," was the admonition of Paul to his spiritual son Timothy. "I have fought the good fight, I have finished the race, I have kept the faith. Finally, there is laid up for me the crown of righteousness, which the Lord, the righteous Judge, will give to me on that Day, and not to me only but also to all who have loved His appearing" (2 Timothy 4:7-8 NKJV).

This came from a man who knew how it felt to push through the muck that accompanies the Christian life, toward the glory to be revealed. Paul reflected on the decades of ministry experiences along with the spiritual and natural wars. Yet, he looked toward his eternal reward, the place reserved for everyone who presses forward, holding onto their faith no matter what, until God orders them home.

We live in a time when Christianity is being attacked by an insidious and devious enemy. Its name is complacency! It is not unlike a virus in the body that attacks weak cells until the healthy cells are infected. The results can be devastating and must be fought against. In the movie *The Patriot*, during the scene depicting the most important battle against the tyrannical British army led by Lord Cornwallis, the revolutionary soldiers begin to retreat. Fighting with the colonials, the French Major Jean Villeneuve yells to Colonel Benjamin Martin, "Colonel, the line is faltering, the line is faltering!" Realizing how important it was that the men didn't give up, Colonel Martin picks up the fallen American flag and runs toward the enemy while waving the flag. Passing his retreating comrades, and running toward the battle, he shouts, "Don't turn back men, no retreat!" This act of leadership caused courage to rise in those running from the battle. Reengaging, the soldiers turned around and returned to the fight. That battle marked the turning point of the Revolutionary War. Ultimately, they won the war and their freedom.

My friends, our line is faltering. If we acknowledge this truth, we can be transformed from weak and timid men of God into the warriors we are called to be. Transformed, we become a people who reflect the spirit of the coming Lord, with the personality and spirit of the lion, not the lamb. I hope this book brings crisis, a turning point for every person who reads it; only through crisis will real people of faith be saved from extinction.

This book is to be a mirror! It will make you mad. It will make you cry. By the end, if you are big enough, it will be life changing. If you navigate this time correctly, you will become an invaluable weapon in God's arsenal. You are not done! Get ready to have your world turned upside down. It is interesting to me that the only thing Christ took with Him in His ascension to heaven were His scars, which speaks volumes. You see, scars are the proof of a life lived right. And our Hero and Lord lived His life to die. The message for you and me is clear. The scars we obtain in the fulfillment of our calling are eternal. We are supposed to arrive in eternity bloodied and scarred when we die. When we do, we will die to see a greater day.

CHAPTER 1

THE FIGHT

"You'll have time to rest when your dead."

Robert De Niro

Jesus' Prayer for His Followers

nd this is the real and eternal life: That they know you, the one and only true God, and Jesus Christ, whom you sent. I glorified you on earth by completing down to the last detail what you assigned me to do. And now, Father, glorify me with your very own splendor, the very splendor I had in your presence before there was a world.

John 17:3-5

This is one of the most powerful and revealing prayers in Scripture. Jesus walks methodically through His own history while on earth, culminating in a good death. He gave us everything, leaving it all on the battlefield of life. He showed us how to fight evil, how to love and also to hate. He guarded those God gave Him. Then He lays out His expectation of our mission, until He comes again. This mission is without ambiguity and cannot be misunderstood. We have a mission, all the power and weapons needed to complete it, and the Spirit of God in us to make sure we are up for each task on the way to completion.

Billy Graham wrote in his book *Angels*, "*We live in a perpetual battlefield...The wars among the nations on earth are mere popgun affairs compared to the fierceness of battle in the spiritual unseen world. This invisible spiritual conflict is waged around us incessantly and unremittingly. Where the Lord works, Satan's forces hinder; where angel beings carry out divine directives, the devils rage. All this comes about because the powers of darkness press their counterattack to recapture the ground held for the glory of God.*"

During the revolution in Ukraine, hundreds of men, women, and young people were gunned down by the forces controlled by the now-deposed President Yanukovych. I was honored to be in those same streets a few days after these atrocities were committed against the heroic Ukrainians. My dear friend Kim Clement, a camera crew, and I traveled there with a desire to weep with those who weep, bring comfort to those we could, and to fight. I witnessed firsthand the pain and suffering in that revolution. I smelled the smells of war, saw the shrines to the dead, and listened and watched as grown men and women wept loudly. Among those fighting in the streets were Christians giving out Bibles, providing for the wounded, and some even dying for freedom. Today we have living examples of this, examples of men rising to the challenge of conflict with boldness and determination.

Crimean pastor Kostya Bakonov found himself in the center of a war between Russian and Ukrainian forces. A pastor who most likely had both Russian and Ukrainian people in his congregation made a decision to get into the fight not with passive platitudes, but with action. In the face of escalating tension and increased media speculation, Bakonov said his motto had become "less news and television, more Bible and prayer."

"Yes, we are concerned about the situation in Crimea, but I encourage our congregation of 800 believers by the Word of God," he said. "I continue to preach the gospel to the people of Crimea and beyond."

Despite constant changes and rising tensions, Bakonov was most concerned for the spiritual outcome of the time of unrest. He was encouraged during the Maidan protests as churches in Kiev ministered in the center of the unrest and helped Ukrainians find peace in the midst of the conflict. He said many people in the country are spiritually open because of the ongoing hostilities. "Many people in Ukraine have been searching for answers and are seeking the answers from churches and ministers. We praise God that He is opening hearts to reveal Himself," Bakonov said.

I remember thinking to myself, if there is any place a Christian should feel completely at home, it is where such things are happening. As days passed, I heard the Lord say something to me that shook me to the core. He said, "The blood of those who die in the faith will always have a voice. A voice that no one can quiet." Then I thought of all the heroes of faith written about by Paul in the book of Hebrews. Their blood still speaks. In fact Paul called them a "cloud of witnesses." AnIn other words, they died to see another day.

Where Men Are Hiding

We do not have to look too far into history to see an example of what real manhood is. In World War II men from their late teens to their forties flocked to protect a nation and fight tyranny. Boys from farms to the big city didn't have to be convinced or coerced to join the military forces and fight. They willingly left weeping parents and ran to the fields and waterways of war. It was not in their DNA to do anything else. And so many died a good death in that war, giving it all so that others could live. But something began to happen to men after that. In the decades since the World Wars, the majority of men have become acclimated to activities that keep them from engagement in righteous conflict. And technology has helped them.

When a person gives their soul to fantasy they effectively surrender to ineptitude. Video gaming companies make billions of dollars producing visuals intended to occupy a person's God-given need to fight evil. Losing oneself in fantasy roles has become a favorite pastime. In 2005, a South Korean man died after a reported 50-hour video gaming session, and in 2012 a Taiwanese man was discovered dead in his gaming chair, arms outstretched for his computer even in the middle of a fatal cardiac arrest.

The apostle Paul said, "When I was a child, I talked like a child, I thought like a child, I reasoned like a child: now that I have become a man, I am done with childish ways and have put them aside." 1 Corinthians 13:11 (AMP).

Then there are the many videos depicting courage in acts against darkness from *Star Wars* to *Transformers*, where men live out their warrior dreams while eating popcorn and candy. As a child, after watching a movie with cowboys and Indians, I would go to the tree and pick a branch in the neighbor's yard and create a bow and arrow. Then I would act out my imaginary fight by running and shooting nonexistent enemies. That is what children do. Not full-grown men.

There is a warrior in every one of us. We were formed with the innate desire to fight. But our fight is not against an imaginary enemy. Our enemy, the one who is adept at creating death, unfortunately is winning. His bounty is the family, our sons and daughters, our marriages, our morality, and our soul. The prophet Joel said in Joel 3:9-10 (ESV), "Proclaim this among the nations: Consecrate for war; stir up the mighty men. Let all the men of war draw near; let them come up. Beat your plowshares into swords, and your pruning hooks into spears; let the weak say, "I am a warrior."

In this prophetic proclamation, heaven initiates the call for change. Uncontaminated and unquenchable, the voice of God speaks through the hearts of His servants, a voice that declares the time is at hand for the weak and the strong to step up and say, "I am a warrior." With this declaration, the realization of imminent war and a lifestyle of regimented discipline become obvious. I find it interesting that the prophet Joel speaks of plowshares and pruning hooks, tools of a farmer. The message here is, "whatever it is you toil and work at, I call you now to refashion it into a weapon of war."

History shows us that change is difficult for the church. Each time change is initiated by God, much of the church stubbornly resists it. I saw the movie *Son of God*, produced by Mark Burnett, and I couldn't help but wonder at the stubbornness of the existing religious system depicted on screen. But at the same time, in a weird way, I understood.

From a human perspective, each of the men who led the Jewish people were used to having their way. For thousands of years things had been done the same way. Then along comes this voice from heaven, the Word of God, Jesus Christ. Jesus came with an unorthodox message and practice; He functioned way outside the ordinary religious traditions of the day. After all, the temple was God's plan and the priesthood was God's method of communicating with the people. And even though Scripture foretold the coming Messiah, the religious system resisted and destroyed the messenger. The change Jesus declared proved difficult to imagine. It required humility and willingness to lose control. People in power often struggle with these attributes. However, to be a hero in our faith and to finish the race we began, there is no more vital characteristic than humility. Humility has always been and will always be a precedent for dynamic heavenly activity.

God's timing is rarely within the scope of our choosing. He is God, and we are His sons and daughters. The happenings in our world are not a surprise to Him. He is all-knowing, all-seeing, and everywhere at once. Who can legitimately question the will of such a being? I must say though, I don't think our loving God really minds if we don't like it, or even that we wrestle with His plans, as long as we always come to the place where we finally embrace it.

Accepting the Unexpected

The country was Indonesia. I traveled there with two friends to speak at several churches before continuing on our trek through Asia. Indonesia is an interesting country. I enjoyed the unique tropical balmy weather. We stayed at a small hotel engulfed in a sea of endless noises. Cars, trucks, buses, and the call to prayer of the mosque's muezzin echoed in the air. Indonesia is the largest Muslim nation on earth; therefore Islam is practiced by the majority. Unlike the Middle East, the people there are by-and-large very kind to foreigners.

There is no feeling of uneasiness or threat because the Asian people are not generally prone to such behavior. But there is a busyness among the people that is necessary for survival. Every single day is a fight for existence and you can see the desperation in their eyes and actions. There is no government subsidy to help them, no unemployment fund, only their ability to make life work. And they do, make it work, any way they can. Such is life in a third world country.

On one particular balmy night, I was the featured speaker at a gathering of hundreds of Christians. I looked forward to speak on my topic: The believer's authority. The building was packed with people, with standing room only. Since I did not speak the language, I had an interpreter. It took some time to develop a cadence with him but once we got in sync the message began to flow. Then it happened! Out of the blue, I sensed the need to stop speaking.

I encouraged those who felt particularly oppressed and unable to grasp the message I was attempting so hard to communicate to come to the front and receive prayer. I glanced over at my companions sitting behind me and made it obvious that I would need their help with prayer. As I turned my head back around, I noticed a massive amount of people streaming forward. About half of the congregation was moving toward me. I remember feeling overwhelmed, but excited at the opportunity to pray for them.

Suddenly, something cold came over me. I looked at the guys behind me and it was clear they felt it too. Both of them were standing with their hands raised in intense prayer. At once and without warning, the place went black. The power to the building went off. When I say black, I mean dark enough so you could not see your hand in front of you!

Since Indonesia is a Muslim nation, whenever Christians meet, especially in large numbers, the windows are closed and the curtains are drawn to protect the identities of the people. For what seemed an eternity, we waited for the power to return. Some passed the time singing, filling the building with songs of worship. Finally, the power returned. At that time, we resumed our invitation to those who wanted special prayer, asking them to move down the aisle for ministry.

After praying for about 15 minutes, something astounding happened. A demon showed up! Standing on the first step of the stage, my attention was diverted. A man among the crowd began to make what I can only describe as the sound of a wild cat. He lay on his back, making this sound for roughly thirty seconds. I looked at the men who were with me with an expression of both terror and confusion. I'm ashamed to admit it, but I was caught by surprise by what I saw and heard. To make matters worse, something totally supernatural took place. The man lying on his back, making the cat noise, started to move his arms in a martial arts manner, while floating. Yes, I said floating! He hovered across the floor.

While this guy floated, I stood there dumbfounded. Since I was clearly not acting, one of my partners decided to make a move. He jumped from the stage, landing on our floating cat guy. My friend began to command the demon to come out. The demon left. The man once stricken with a horrible invader was now free and lying motionless. Then his eyes opened, absent the crazed look, and with a tangible peace he stood to the cheers of the people.

Mesmerized, I stood there and watched the whole thing! Try to picture the scene. Here is the so-called "man of God," who moments before was teaching on the believer's authority, unengaged in the battle against a demonic force. Later that evening, I spoke with a few local church leaders. They shared information that helped me understand what I experienced that night. They explained that men will embody the spirit of a fierce animal, a lion or a panther, to make them more effective in martial arts. Upon reflection, I recognized that while I was speaking, the Holy Spirit decided to pick a fight with the demons in the room. It is hard to admit, but I wasn't up for the fight.

My reluctance to engage the enemy in Indonesia was a defining moment for me. I realized that the preaching of the gospel, when done under the anointing of God, is like a stick in the eye to all the forces of darkness. Demons have no power that can withstand the name of Jesus or those who are used to free those captive by them. When believers willingly place themselves in service to God's agenda He always backs them up with the power of the One who saw a good death and lived to see another day. The name of Jesus cripples Satan and his demons, causing them to panic, which is revealed in the convulsions of the oppressed. A demon will do anything to maintain its hold.

Unlike the examples of movies like *The Exorcist*, demons are not only subject to those who are considered clergy. They are subject to any believer who is prepared to deal with them. After this encounter, I determined it was my duty to never again be unprepared to encounter the enemy. I understood by making that decision, I would be required to live a vastly different life than the one I had lived up to that point. War was staring me in the face; I needed to be ready, equipped, and willing to fight to the finish.

My Journey

Born into a poor family, my life, like many struggling families, was a mixture of ups and downs, but mostly downs. My parents worked hard and saved every penny. They did whatever possible to meet our needs. I watched my dad work two jobs for his entire life. Each day he rose at three in the morning, and with his thermos and steel lunch bucket in hand, he headed to work at the factory. Dad was a tool and die maker. On most days, he came home with fresh scars on his arms due to molten metal hitting his flesh while doing his job.

After working all day at the factory, he came home and quickly dressed in his barber's smock. Then he would leave for work again, this time at his barbershop. Dad cut hair with his partner, an old bald man, ironically named, Curly. Dad barbered until closing time, usually around eight o'clock. Arriving home, he ate the dinner my mom always had waiting for him, and then went directly to bed. That was his daily routine, except for Sundays. Sunday was the only day Dad did not work.

Every Sunday morning, Dad woke my two brothers, my sister and me up for church. We attended mass at Saint Mary's Catholic Church in Fullerton, California. Dad made it clear that he expected us to sit perfectly still through all the religious activities. After some time I was made an altar boy at Saint Mary's. I thought being an altar boy was better than sitting through the religious service.

In my view, every mass was like someone pushed the replay button and the priests and the people repeated the liturgy on cue. That attitude guaranteed trouble for me with just about everyone. Saint Mary's was also my school for eight long years. Dad demanded that we all go to a private Catholic school instead of a public one. I am uncertain as to why, but my dad had a serious attitude about public education. He didn't trust the public school system to educate his kids.

Dad was born on a farm in Adair, Iowa. From a young age, he worked long, hard hours in the cornfields. He didn't enjoy farm life. So at the age of seventeen, with only a tenth grade education, he joined the army. Soon after his enlistment, he deployed to Korea. Dad never really talked about what happened to him during the war, but from the scars on his body, we all knew he experienced something awful there. It wasn't until my father's funeral, I finally learned the significance of his scars. Wally, my dad's best friend, attended his graveside service. Wally was not just a friend; he saved my father's life in combat. Wally spoke to me briefly about the battle in which dad sustained his wounds: "A whole lot of good men died that day!" I knew if I pressed him for more information he would lose his composure so I chose to leave it alone.

My dad was a good father in the sense that he provided for us. But on other parental matters, he was rather detached. Not much for talking, Dad kept his thoughts and words to himself. My father displayed a bold confidence so I always felt secure in his presence. When he was nearby, I knew nothing could hurt me. There is a common remembrance shared by all of my dad's childhood friends: Dad was a fighter! I can testify of his fighting spirit as well. Dad was short in stature, but thick and strong as an ox.

I remember one time he took us to the motorcycle races. My two brothers and I sat close to the track for a better view. For some reason, Dad decided to sit with a friend a few rows above us. We were just being kids, but our antics bugged this older guy sitting behind us. I suppose the man had enough, as he grabbed my brother by the collar and started yelling at him. Suddenly, and without warning, my dad picked the man up and threw him onto the racetrack, right in the middle of a race.

Afterward, Dad calmly returned to his seat, as if nothing happened. The rest of the night went without incident. However, for my brothers and me, we felt we had Superman as a father. We relished the experience of a fearless father. That night each of us beamed with pride at his antics. If trouble came to us my dad was never far off. If we were wrong, he let us reap the consequences. But if we were not, it was going to be a bad day for whoever wronged us.

Mom was the light of our home. I still remember her constant encouragement and saintly presence. I cannot remember ever waking up in the night or being in need of her when she didn't suddenly show up. As a young child I used to have night terrors. I would scream and thrash around and have no memory of what happened. The next morning my mom would make me a special breakfast for just the two of us. During breakfast she would tell me in a soft caring way that I had a bad dream. She would gently ask if there was anything that I knew of that would give her insight into helping me.

Mom could make life feel good even if all we had was a tent to live in. To help bring income into the household, my mother attended beauty school. Upon graduation, dad built her a small salon in the foyer of our house. She refused to work outside the home. She wanted to be home for her family. Almost every day, women came to have their hair done. Those were the days when women had "high hair." They would come to the house with flat heads and leave with hair that touched the roof of their cars. When mom was not styling a woman's hair, she was busy cooking in the kitchen.

We didn't have money to buy bread or fresh milk. Therefore, Mom baked our bread; she made just about everything from scratch. Our milk did not come in a bottle or carton, but in a box. We were given horrible powered milk, which to me tasted like sandy water. She also had a vegetable garden in the front yard. During the day, when she had a moment to spare, you would find her tending it. I remember her persistent invitations to sit with her on the ground and eat her tomatoes like most people eat apples. Mom was very encouraging; I can't recall ever hearing her say anything negative. I depended on her approval and affirmation as I faced the challenges of my youth. Every word she spoke to me was filled with kindness and loving motivation. Our life was good, even though it seemed to be a constant struggle. In a weird way, I am glad that I was born without any leg up in life. I learned life isn't kind and if I wanted to succeed in life I needed to win battles.

At the young age of 37, my mom died from a rare disease called scleroderma. The disease was torturous and very rare. But my mother was a fighter. She would not allow this disease, which essentially turns a person into stone, to define her. For more than two years she faced the unbearable pain and lived for us. Among her last words were, "God, please don't let me die, I want to be with my children."

She died fighting. She died a good death. I was 13 years old. From the moment of her death, my siblings and I were thrown into a fight for survival. Devastated by mother's death, Dad turned inward and he rarely communicated with us. As a result, we learned to fend for ourselves. We had a roof over our heads. But we were responsible to provide for our other basic needs. Any money we had, we earned. We would either search for bottles and redeem them or work at a car wash in town. There were no handouts from my dad.

My siblings and I were never encouraged to go to college or achieve anything great in life. There were no little league games, no Boy Scouts, nothing extracurricular. As a young man, I spent most of my free time at the Boys Club, playing pool and hanging out. When I was a junior at Fullerton High School, my dad told me he was holding a place for me at the factory where he worked. One Saturday, he took me to the factory and showed me what he did for work. He took pride in his job, although secretly, I wondered why. One thing I knew for sure, I would never work there. Truth is, seeing his work place helped motivate me to attend college.

Years later, my father contracted lung disease, which ultimately took his life. He was 63 years old when he died. A few days before he passed away, he told me something that I will never forget. He said, "Son, make something of your life! Don't die without leaving your mark and don't expect anything to be given to you. You will have to fight for every inch but when you are where I am now, believe me, you don't want to regret the life you lived." After saying those words, he moved onto the business at hand, making me the executor of his small estate, and explaining to me how he wanted things to be handled when he passed. Two weeks later, at home in his bed, he died of congestive heart failure. His regret in the life he lived underscored the fact that he didn't die a good death. He died with many regrets and unfulfilled dreams. His last words to me resonate to this day.

Not long after his death I made a commitment to God that I would do everything possible not to waste my life by refusing to live in the smallness of my mind and insecurities. A few years prior to my father's death, I accepted Christ, which insured that I could actually keep my commitment. From the very moment Jesus Christ came into my life, my purpose was ignited. The fogginess of life no longer had any power over me. My decision to live a life worth living, and to fight any resistance either within or without, was bolstered by the agreement coming from heaven.

This was not an oath made out of the emotion of a moment, but out of the work of the Holy Spirit working through an imperfect man. It has been many years since that moment. Today, one single fact remains clear to me: Life is a fight! Acknowledging this truth and applying it determines either my success or failure. When you forget that life is war, you get hammered! To stay at the top of your game, you must engage the battlefields of life. As long as you stay in the fight, your destiny will find you.

"Your God has commanded your strength [your might in His service and impenetrable hardness to temptation]; O God, display Your might and strengthen what You have wrought for us!" Psalm 68:28 (AMP).

The Warrior's Touch

As our enemies have found we can reason like men, so now let us show them we can fight like men also." **Thomas Jefferson**

One of the inspirations behind the writing of this book came when I was challenged to write a eulogy for my brother-in-law and spiritual mentor who died of bone cancer at the young age of 56. He died a good death. As I penned his tribute, it soon became clear that my words we not completely my own, the Holy Spirit invaded my thoughts. Through this interaction, I was led to move beyond trivial and typical words, to deep, meaningful, and long-lasting communication. Just God and me, an equation for revelation.

Let me interject a note of truth here. God is not somewhere out there, in the ethereal soup, untouchable and generally aloof to men and their plights. Through the Holy Spirit, He is reachable, and through faith, He will interact with anyone who seeks Him. During my life's journey, I have been blessed to know how to discern the moments when God is working through me. If you have experienced it, you know exactly what I mean; if you have not, then simply ask for it and expect it.

I vividly remembered that difficult season when I didn't have the slightest idea of what my purpose was in life. Then suddenly, God's agent, my brother-in-law Rick, was sent to be the first to guide me onto the path. As I wrote, I realized how blessed I was to be mentored by so many amazing people. Distinct individuals sent to me at strategic times, people who refused to allow me to live my life as anything less than a warrior. Some stood alongside me for a season, while others are still walking with me.

Among them are my wife, Amber; my late brother-in-law, Rick Lane; the man of wisdom, Dr. Edwin Louis Cole; pastor Chuck Smith; Gary Greenwald; my fellow warrior and lifelong friend, Kim Clement; and a true apostle in the faith, pastor Steve Murrell. These individuals were the vessels God used to pull me onto the path He had chosen for me. They were not placed in my life by mistake; they were purposefully positioned in my life by loving, divine leading. They were sent to communicate God's wisdom to me, each in their unique way, and among other things, to remind me that life is war. Always war! Their examples taught me that I was not going to have the option of shunning it either.

In Rick's eulogy I wrote, "Rick was family, but more than that, he was the first man God placed in my life to help me see as God sees." The interesting thing about Rick was that he wasn't this bombastic man who threw his opinion around with pomposity. He did most of his talking without talking. At his funeral, in my tribute to him, I noted that Rick well understood our unique creative design. God gave us two ears while only giving us one mouth, making sure we knew He wanted us to do twice as much listening as speaking. Rick was a listener, rarely if ever verbose. Through patience and long-suffering, Rick was able to hear not only what we said, but, more importantly, that which wasn't said.

He could read the heart better than anyone I knew. It was this ability that made him so valuable to those who loved him.

I didn't spend a lot of time with Rick in my 30-plus years of knowing him, but the times we did spend together remain a lasting memory. Focused and giving his undivided attention, he was fully there. Every time he left his unique form of wisdom in me, moving me to a greater place of commitment to a life that matters. If I were to note one thing Rick underscored to me, it would be this: we are always at war. There is something uniquely astounding about a person who deeply touches a life in very few words and with little time spent. To have this effect reveals a constitution of the soul, a seasoned warrior.

We live in a world today devoid of people like Rick. The world lacks men and women with the constitution of a warrior. A true and devoted warrior never takes a day off from battle or at the very least, the training and equipping for it. Seasoned warriors are a rare breed; they not only lead by example but they are motivated by the urgent call to enlist others in the fight. The aimlessness of humanity reveals that these elite characteristics are in short supply today. It is high time for that to change.

A.W. Tozer said, *"We languish for men who feel themselves expendable in the warfare of the soul because they have died to the allurements of the world. Such men will be free from the compulsions that control weaker men. They will not be forced to do things by the squeeze of circumstances. Their only compulsion will come from within or from above."*

It is time to enter the battlefield, for it is on the field of battle you find out who you really are. Real engagement in the activity of fighting for others and sacrificing your life for the man next to you will reveal the real you. In the movie *Blackhawk Down* there is a scene where the men have just returned to safety, bloodied and bruised. Soon the order came down from the general to have all the men return back to the battle.

One of the men disclosed to another, "I can't go back. I can't do that again." His brother Ranger looked back to him and said, "Thomas, we all feel the same way you do. But it is what you do right now that will define you. Make your decision." The next scene shows the troops loaded up in the Humvees, less Thomas. But Thomas sees the face of his friend peering back to him in the side mirror. With seconds left before the troops leave him, courage fills his being and he runs to the vehicle and reengages the battle. You see, it is not wrong to be afraid, or to even feel like quitting. What is wrong is to allow those emotions to define you. That is why we need others. You cannot do it alone! You cannot do it as an army of one!

There is no way to reach the place where God wants you to be unless you understand the warrior's touch. This is an event that changes the course of a man's life. This touch is never the result of hype. The warrior's touch comes uninvited and without notice through another man or woman who once experienced the same touch. It is not subject to popular trend, but is often the initiator of a new one. The warrior's touch is seen throughout scripture hundreds of times. From the moment Elijah threw his mantel on Elisha, to the choosing of the twelve disciples, the warrior's touch can be clearly identified. You may experience this many times in a lifetime. Personally, I can point to a handful of times when it has happened to me.

It is one thing to acknowledge that we are at war but it's another thing to become equipped to enter the fight. One of the most important parts of the equipping process is the warrior's touch. Without that touch, you have a big void, one I'm sure you already realize. You are the proverbial round peg in the square hole. In the deepest recesses of your heart this torturing frustration taunts you. I don't care who you are, even if you consider yourself "self made," you are not complete if you cannot identify those moments when God used another person as a directing force in your life. Sadly, there are not enough of those experienced in warfare that are capable or qualified to be the hand of God on your shoulder. But there are multitudes that will do the opposite. The majority of people in the world are not walking in their "God spot."

Only a man who is standing in his "God spot" can call another to it. In his timing God sends wise, seasoned, and scarred men to us. When they touch you, crisis ensues, which is common to a warrior. Crisis should be celebrated because it means that God is active in the warrior's life. It should never be disdained; the true warrior always meets his crisis with a "bring it on" attitude!

Most of the people I work with are in some form of military service, and some of them are special forces or special operations. For more than a decade, it has been my pleasure to mentor many SEALs (Sea, Air & Land teams) on spiritual matters. Repeatedly, I watched them enter BUD/S (Basic Underwater Demolition/SEAL training) as young men and then graduate transformed as warriors. At every graduation the SEAL ethos is read. This ethos is written on the hearts of every one of the graduating men. I have attended dozens of graduations and noticed that many of the new SEALs mouth the ethos as it is read from the podium.

"In times of war or uncertainty there is a special breed of warrior ready to answer our Nation's call. A common man with uncommon desire to succeed. Forged by adversity, he stands alongside America's finest special operations forces to serve his country, the American people, and protect their way of life. I am that man.

My Trident is a symbol of honor and heritage. Bestowed upon me by the heroes that have gone before, it embodies the trust of those I have sworn to protect. By wearing the Trident I accept the responsibility of my chosen profession and way of life. It is a privilege that I must earn every day. My loyalty to Country and Team is beyond reproach. I humbly serve as a guardian to my fellow Americans always ready to defend those who are unable to defend themselves. I do not advertise the nature of my work, nor seek recognition for my actions. I voluntarily accept the inherent hazards of my profession, placing the welfare and security of others before my own. I serve with honor on and off the battlefield. The ability to control my emotions and my actions, regardless of circumstance, sets me apart from other men. Uncompromising integrity is my standard. My character and honor are steadfast. My word is my bond. We expect to lead and be led. In the absence of orders, I will take charge, lead my teammates and accomplish the mission. I lead by example in all situations. I will never quit. I persevere and thrive on adversity. My Nation expects me to be physically harder and mentally stronger than my enemies. If knocked down, I will get back up, every time. I will draw on every remaining ounce of strength to protect my teammates and to accomplish our mission. I am never out of the fight. We demand discipline. We expect innovation. The lives of my teammates and the success of our mission depend on me—my technical skill, tactical proficiency, and attention to detail. My training is never complete.

We train for war and fight to win. I stand ready to bring the full spectrum of combat power to bear in order to achieve my mission and the goals established by my country. The execution of my duties will be swift and violent when required yet guided by the very principles that I serve to defend.

Brave men have fought and died building the proud tradition and feared reputation that I am bound to uphold. In the worst of conditions, the legacy of my teammates steadies my resolve and silently guides my every deed. I will not fail!"

When I hear this ethos read at each graduation, I cannot help but think of the book of Hebrews and the words of Paul the apostle: "We are surrounded by a cloud of witnesses." These witnesses are the men and women who lived in times past and paved the way. These men and women are the embodiment of what a warrior is supposed to look like. Their lives declared that there is an expectation handed down to carry on the traditions set forth. Courage, commitment, sacrifice, and duty are the core of that tradition. Warfare was the inescapable reality they each faced with determination and poise.

Christians have a cloud of witnesses, men and women in the heavens watching to see if we will pony up to the battle. Christianity and spiritual warfare are not mutually exclusive. These go hand-in-hand and one cannot have faith in Christ without experiencing spiritual warfare. Any attempt to avoid it will result in losing faith. The apostle Paul said something striking in the first chapter of the letter to the Roman church, "First, I thank God through Jesus Christ for you all, that your faith is spoken of throughout the whole world" (Romans 1:8). When you are observed by others, is there evidence of faith? As you continue to read let that be your heart's meditation.

CHAPTER 2

WARFARE IS A GIVEN

*"I was only the servant of my country and had I, at any moment,
failed to express her unflinching resolve to fight and conquer, I
should at once have been rightly cast aside."*

Winston Churchill

It was a sunny Super Bowl Sunday; excitement was in the air as I arrived at church to speak at both services. People in the parking lot were talking about the various ways they were going to watch the game. Some of them were wearing their team's shirts or hats. I quickly realized that church was not on the forefront of their minds and I have to admit it wasn't on mine either. As I preached my message that day, I saw something in the eyes of the people that I can only describe as a "make the sermon quick" look. Since I too was a huge football fan, I was glad to accommodate them.

While speaking, I noticed a man sitting on the front row of the right side of the building. He kind of stuck out. I kept thinking to myself that he looked like a SEAL. Let me explain. Once you have worked with these warriors for a while, you begin to notice their unique mannerisms—conduct that is typical to them and them only. It's hard to explain, but if you know what to look for you will recognize the demeanor that sets a SEAL apart from others. There is something in the way they carry themselves, something in their eyes, and something in their stoicism that makes them stand out.

One time I was in a restaurant having dinner with my wife, when about 10 men walked in and took their seats. Each of them had some sort of facial hair, and other than their obvious physical fitness, they didn't look like military men. I leaned over the table and told my wife, "those guys are SEALS," and she laughed at me. After a while I heard a woman at another table ask them what they did and why they were in town. One guy answered that they were professional treasure hunters. That sealed (pun intended) it for me! As we were leaving, I asked one of the guys if they were "team guys," (a term usually known only to other SEALs), and he said, "yes." For the rest of the night, I enjoyed ribbing my wife that I was right.

Anyway, back to Super Bowl Sunday, this particular man seemed oblivious to just about everything I said. When I told a joke, he didn't join the rest of the congregation in laughter. When I told a moving story, he remained unmoved. When we sang, he just sat there looking straight ahead. At the close of the message, I invited anyone who didn't know Christ to come forward after the meeting for prayer. I have to admit, he was the last guy I thought would respond to my invitation.

But when I dismissed the congregation, he was the first one to meet me. With the same stoic look he had on his face the entire service, he told me that he wanted to accept Christ "right now!" As would be expected, I gladly prayed with him. With deep sincerity, he repeated the words asking Christ to forgive his sins and accepted Jesus Christ as Lord. When we finished praying, I gave him a Bible and directions to our new believers class being held the next night. I kind of expected that to be it for the day, but we were not done.

I am going to jump ahead here, and give you some background information on Steve, our new believer. Months after

Super Bowl Sunday, I learned from the other SEALs attending the church that Steve had quite a reputation as a SEAL. Steve was a harsh and brutal warrior. During his long career, he had seen some horrific combat and had conducted himself with distinction on the battlefield. Steve was a feared, but deeply respected, Special Operations professional.

When Steve came to our church, he was an instructor at BUD/S or Basic Underwater Demolitions/Seal training center, in Coronado, California. His students gave him the name "Satan" because of how hard he was on them during training. As I look back on that day, I have to laugh. When Steve arrived at church that day, the BUD/S students in attendance moved to the other side of the building. I believe they were attempting to stay as far away from "Satan" as possible.

Okay, back to Super Bowl Sunday. In all my years of ministry, I cannot think of another experience that compares with what happened next. Steve looked at me and said, "I need to be baptized." I commended him for his desire and told him that we would be glad to baptize him, if he would call the office and schedule it. He just stared at me without a flinch and stated emphatically, "You don't understand. I want to be baptized now!" He went on to say that in three hours he would be waiting for me at the pool on the naval base. At this point, he gave me the address, confirmed that I had access to the base, turned, and walked away.

As Steve exited, a group of people immediately came up to me, asking me to join them at their various parties. Still a little bit in shock, I told them thank you, but I had another commitment and I could not change it. On the way home, my wife, a huge football fan, asked me where we were going to watch the game. When I recounted my experience, she replied with understandable chagrin, "Well, it looks like I will be watching the game by myself!" I made my apology, found my bathing suit, and headed back to the naval base on Coronado Island.

When I arrived at the pool, I expected to meet Steve, go through the teaching on baptism, and then baptize him. What I found was nothing less than astounding. In the three hours between our meeting at the pulpit and that moment, Steve had gathered three other SEALs. He told them about his conversion and the change that he was already experiencing due to his profession of faith. Boldly, Steve invited each of them to participate in the baptism. That day I was able to pray with those SEALs and each accepted Christ and were baptized.

This all happened because one man refused to be put off. To Steve, truth demanded action NOW! There is one more thing about Steve I must tell you. After the baptism, Steve took me aside and thanked me for showing up. Then he asked me something astounding, "Do we get to fight?" I had never had anybody ask me that question. Even though the Scriptures are full of stories and admonitions to fight evil, I had never once heard this question uttered.

My response to him was an immediate yes, yet to be completely honest, in my heart I wasn't sure what that really meant. I have to admit that until I was challenged by Steve, I didn't think of spiritual warfare as anything but the acts of prayer and binding the devil. But Steve represented to me a new form of believer, one who is birthed into the kingdom of God with the innate desire, not only to love Jesus, but also to fight against His enemies. These believers are beginning to surface now all over the world. Birthed with the spirit of the warrior, their task is to shake the church to a place of readiness, to prepare the way for the coming Lion of Judah and to be equipped to fight all His enemies.

After my encounter with Steve, I spent several months studying the idea of warfare in the believer's life. There is a devil, and there are demons, and there are evil people under their control. Mankind continues to become more and more evil. The innocent are targets even in the womb. Human trafficking is now a 32 billion dollar industry. Child trafficking for sex and labor is growing worldwide. Perversion is increasing and evil grows. All of this would be depressing if I was not aware of who Jesus is and who He destined me to be.

I live now! Today is my time! I am reminded of the admonition of Luke 19:13 where Jesus admonishes the stewards of his talents to "occupy until I come." This literally means to busy oneself. Nowhere in Scripture are we encouraged to sit around and do nothing. In my many years of being a Christian, I have noticed a great deal of attention given to the Rapture. I have lived to see great men of God actually give dates for Christ's return. I have a hard time understanding this because we are clearly told we will not know the time or the season of Christ's return.

One reason for this withholding is the minute we think we know when Christ returns we will stop changing the world. And something else really bothers me about the escapists who declare a date for the coming of the Lord. The poor people who were duped into believing their lie and sold their belongings, quit their jobs, and separated from the call God placed on them, heard nothing when the predicted time came and went. No apology, nothing!

And those who believed are left with a hole in them, feeling foolish, and disenchanted with the church. A real leader would have repented to those who were fooled. Then he would help them get back into the fight of life through example, being the first to step up and fight for the weak, being an agent of God in darkness with a vow to never again be duped into such deceptions.

A Natural Counterpart

Jesus said that there will always be wars and rumors of war. Example after example are related in the Bible. In fact, I cannot think of a single battle written in the Bible that does not have both a spiritual and a natural component. The men and women were called by God to carry out God's vengeance on the enemy and to deal with physical death and destruction as a result of God's order to engage darkness.

When young David arrived on the battlefield in the valley of Shochoh, he was not aware that his entire world was about to change. You might surmise that he was like many of us today. He could have felt insecure about himself. As the youngest of his brothers and the one who was always ignored, David could have been somewhat depressed, feeling like his life was of little value. But on this appointed day, David's destiny was going to be revealed.

Isn't it interesting that his complete version of the man he was made to be happened because he committed himself to the battle. Furthermore, David didn't just stand there and pray. He mocked Goliath, and then stepped forward to physically attack him. Do you see? The equation of war was this: God gave His direction, a man followed it, and evil was decimated.

Today, not enough believers get into the fight for the soul of society. This is due to what I call the feminization of the church. This term is not to disparage females; rather, I want to convey the message that people in the church are not engaged in a manner of readiness and preparedness. Men no longer train for war. Demands are not made of us by those speaking from the pulpits or from ourselves. We are so busy fighting the fight within that we never get to a place of readiness to fight the fight without.

We are engaged in the twenty-first century pastime of navel gazing. We are inward focused, diagnosing ourselves with depression, reliving past pain, and finding excuses for inaction. The Centers for Disease Control and Prevention has classified prescription drug abuse as an epidemic. While there has been a marked decrease in the use of some illegal drugs like cocaine, data from the National Survey on Drug Use and Health (NSDUH) show that nearly one-third of people aged 12 and over who used drugs for the first time in 2009 began by using a prescription drug non-medically.

Some individuals who misuse prescription drugs, particularly teens, believe these substances are safer than illicit drugs because they are prescribed by a healthcare professional and dispensed by a pharmacist. Addressing the prescription drug abuse epidemic is not only a top priority for public health, it will also help build stronger communities and allow those with substance abuse disorders to lead healthier, more productive lives.

It is interesting to me that our youth are the most vulnerable to prescription drug abuse. Can this be due to the lack of direction they see in the church today? Our young people are looking for a fight, one that will engage them in Christ's cause for this age. Several years ago I began to work with an organization that deals with child sex slavery. We held walks intended to make communities aware of what was happening not only in some other country but in our cities in America.

Thousands attended these walks and we were successful at helping people see that trafficking not only happened around them, but they could do something about it. I was not surprised when the students on many college campuses were among the first to step up to action. Thousands of students marched among their fellow students demanding a stop to the abuse of child sex slavery. To this day human trafficking is one of the most talked about causes on our campuses.

Our youth are an easy target today as we marginalize their zeal. We just smile at their causes, making the judgment that when they grow up they will become balanced and be more like us. We hold them back with such judgments and the result is they attempt to put out their fire with drugs. We need to do more in the church than to have youth retreats and beach days. We need to stir up our youth and let them know that part of their identity will be found the same way David found his—by entering the fight.

The Centurion

Some today believe that with His sacrifice, Christ not only ushered in salvation to all mankind but also a new dispensation of pacifism to all believers. I will deal more about this in later chapters. In my study of the bible I cannot find a single time when Christ exhorted those who serve in military service to put down their arms. In fact, He went to great measures to do just the opposite.

Read Matthew 8:5-10: Now when Jesus had entered Capernaum, a centurion came to Him, pleading with Him saying, "Lord, my servant is lying at home paralyzed, dreadfully tormented." And Jesus said to him, "I will come and heal him." The centurion answered and said, "Lord, I am not worthy that You should come under my roof. But only speak a word, and my servant will be healed. For I also am a man under authority, having soldiers under me. And I say to this one, 'Go,' and he goes; and to another, 'Come,' and he comes; and to my servant, 'Do this,' and he does it." When Jesus heard it, He marveled and said to those who followed, "Assuredly I say to you, I have not found such great faith, not even in Israel."

Most people don't realize in the reading of this passage that Christ is delivering an indictment of the religious system of that day. A contemporary paraphrase of His words would sound something like this: "The kind of faith I see in this military officer is a faith I don't see in the church today. What this military man is showing me is what should be present in each of you." In essence, Christ was saying there is something in the character of the warrior that He wants in His church. I for one, will not be put off, nor will I put things off that can be done today. If there seems to be no way, then I will make a way. I will conduct my life in such a manner that mediocrity has no place.

During my decades in ministry, I found that most people join a church for reasons that cannot be substantiated in comparison to the early church. It is understandable when we look at the turbulence in the world. The world can be a depressing place no matter what your standing is. Most people want a controlled environment with great music, cathartic communication, and people acting nice around them for at least one hour in their week.

They want the talks to bring them peace and to make sense of the world. They want to connect with God as long as God doesn't ask too much of them. The problem is many of our churches give them this very thing. In fact many have fallen so far that they are no longer standing for the truth versus what pleases people and their lifestyles. Filling the seats is the main goal and we want people to be happy and without pressure.

The problem is we are not the head of the church. We have no right to do Jesus a favor and change the DNA of the church because we want to keep people happy. Jesus intended the church to be a place of equipping men and women with a soldier's faith. Jesus taught us to run into the battle not from it. Through His example, he taught us to stare down evil and hate it as God does. Giving your all in the exchange against darkness, knowing it may cost you everything is a tenet of our holy faith.

The heavens are crying out to men of God to quit putting off the call to engage the pressure of true discipleship. We live in times when we will either be engaged in the fight of the ages or we will be victims of it. The following is an old Viking code: "When my day comes to die, I will not beg for more time, nor will I cry. I have led a life filled with love and glory. My hope is that I leave this world with a smile on my face and the courage to sing my own death song."

We are Christian men. We have the answer to every issue known to man because we have the risen savior living in us. We are able to do all things through Christ who strengthens us. He has not given us a spirit of fear, but of power, love, and a sound mind. Manhood defined is Christlikeness. Our call is to live on our feet, not die on our knees. That is how men of God speak. This is their code. It is their cry of rebellion against the god of this world.

Spiritual warfare will always be an issue as long as mankind lives on this earth. I define spiritual warfare as the fight against the desires and strategies of darkness. Spiritual warfare is the initiator of all human conflict, which has caused men to commit unconscionable acts against his fellow citizen. Every natural conflict between men, whether it be combat operations between two countries or race wars among men of different colors, is due to the enemy of all men. The enemy, with his insatiable hunger to take a growing abundance of souls into the abyss, is at the bottom of it all. It is clear he will not cease his actions until he faces Christ again as promised in the book of Revelations.

It has been said that spiritual warfare is the underlying apologetic to all theology. This of course began the minute Satan was cast out of heaven along with one-third of the angels. From that moment Satan began to corrupt all that God created. Along with his dark fallen angels he set out to destroy all that is good and beautiful.

To bring strife among men who then terrorize one another. To bring racial war to different ethnicities, causing men to hate one another simply for the color of his skin. To create false religion with tenets of faith that include justification of heinous and brutal murder of the innocent. To create hunger and starvation, the murder of children even in the womb. To create slavery, brutalizing men and women throughout history. To create perversion and sex slavery. This is what Satan has created.

Everywhere you find this ugliness you will find demons, principalities, powers, and evil imps lingering. They are fallen spiritual beings and unless they are faced and made to leave they will continue to reap havoc on the innocent. When we become Christians, we are given power and authority over evil. We are told to use this power and authority first to free ourselves from whatever power the enemy of our soul has over us.

We can't stop there. We are linked to that war whether we like it or not. Today we are either engaged in the battle with Christ and feeling the pressure of battle or we are wandering spiritually and naturally in an existence that has little meaning. A historical study of warfare among men can reveal to us a great deal on this topic.

The fall of the Roman Empire tells us that the most powerful adversary is not necessarily the one with the largest army or most sophisticated weapons. Victory is the byproduct of being on the right side of the conflict. If you believe in God then you must adhere to the truth that all the affairs of men have a predestined outcome. Simply put, nothing is a surprise to God! To follow this thinking one must conclude that God has a side in warfare.

The eminent theologian, C.S. Lewis, wrote the following in his book *Mere Christianity*:

"War is a dreadful thing; I can respect an honest pacifist, though I think he is entirely mistaken. What I cannot understand is this sort of semi-pacifism you get nowadays, which gives people the idea that though you have to fight, you ought to do it with a long face and as if you were ashamed of it."

Dr. Darrell Cole, the assistant professor of religion at Drew University, argues that war is not merely a "necessary evil." Instead, he writes, it's sometimes the right thing for a Christian to do. My view is that war is the only thing to do, beginning with spiritual warfare. War brings out the best and the worst in man and nothing so defines and reveals us as the battle and war. We will either be the man on the run from the bloodiness of battle or we will be the one that runs into the fray, sword raised high having placed our future in the providence of God as many have before us.

The first created man, Adam, entered this world with every blessing possible. He and his wife Eve were surrounded with the best God could give them, including unhindered access to His presence. But the first time they faced true spiritual warfare, Adam shamefully lost without so much as a struggle. Take note that the Bible also ends with a battle, one Christ, the second Adam, wins. In order for you to imbibe the spirit of the second Adam you must begin the transition from an identity with the first Adam, to one with the second Adam, the only savior of man, Jesus Christ.

Several years ago I was invited to a friend's church and asked to teach a series about the biblical figure of Absalom. My friend wanted someone other than himself to communicate to his congregation about this tragic figure in Scripture. Absalom ruined his life because he chose to be on the wrong side of the battle. At one point, I decided to contrast Absalom with another biblical figure named Joseph.

It was interesting that these two men had many similarities. Each was called, gifted, and set up for greatness. Each was reported to have great physical attributes. Each one had a royal heritage. Both experienced a circumstance in their life out of their control. The difference between Absalom and Joseph: one stayed in God's fight while the other became God's fight.

Joseph could not have had a more difficult set of circumstances placed on him. He had every excuse possible to leave the fight. But there was something in him that told him that staying in the fight was the only way for him to achieve his destiny. Absalom, on the other hand, threw away his heritage and died a violent and shameful death. Joseph refused to give it up no matter the cost.

The distinguishing results: Joseph fulfilled his godly purpose while Absalom died a frustrated and defeated man. Joseph NEVER gave up fighting the battle for God's plan. Absalom traded God's plan for his own, a problem that has plagued the church since its beginning.

We were made to follow the path of those who stay in God's fight. Tragically though, many of those who call themselves Christians have never experienced God's fight. Therefore part of the experience of Christianity is missing, leaving us with a void revealing itself in a nagging sense of emptiness. The moment we become believers and accept Christ, we are supposed to see ourselves through the victory of Christ. In today's church, too many believers maintain the passive spirit of the first Adam. When the enemy of our soul comes along, we just remain ambivalent and let him roll over us. The second Adam did just the opposite. Jesus went out and searched for His enemy. And when He found him He essentially told him to do your worst. And Satan tried EVERYTHING with complete failure.

From the beginning of Christ's ministry He made it clear that not only was He not afraid of the devil and his minions, but He would be the worst nightmare of them during the totality of His life as well as His eternal life. And then, at a time reserved only for the Lord Himself, He would return as a Lion with a sword to finish off Satan. That is the resolve of the mighty. And what about us? What do we take away from this indisputable truth? What should this example mean to us? It means that we have a choice. Be like Christ or be like Adam. Which one represents you best?

Have you ever noticed that we love heroes as long as they don't get too close to us? In the movie *Braveheart*, change didn't occur in Scotland until the hero William Wallace forced himself into the midst of the "Nobles." These men loved to have their titles, wealth, and prestige, but they had no will to fight. Every time the tyrant English king wanted to take more freedom from them, they responded by making a truce. William Wallace, a man of no nobility, rose up in their midst and valiantly rode onto the battlefield and picked a fight!

Peace does not come through a truce, It comes through victory. The Nobles were perfectly happy making truces with the enemy. However, the warrior Wallace determined that no matter how outmatched he was in battle, he would never accept a truce with the tyrant king, Longshanks, because a truce accepted the status quo.

It is interesting that Wallace's heroism brought the fight back into the Scottish people. It gave them hope and a reason to live. It caused them to regain their dignity and honor. Tragically, in the end, it was not Longshanks that defeated Wallace, but the vacillating Nobles who felt it better to get rid of the champion among them.

If Wallace were gone, their way would no longer be so obvious. Wallace forced them to either accept the battle, or get out of the way. We need more Wallaces in the world today, especially in the church; men who will accept the call to turn and face the enemies that too long have had their way. To be effective as a warrior it is necessary that we address certain realities.

The Cost

"The more you sweat in training the less you bleed in war."
Sergeant Randy D. Pittman

Most of us become Christians because of the free gift of grace that God gives in order for us to become His child. And that is one of the wonders of God, that He would allow us entry into His family because of Jesus' finished work for us on the cross. But the free gift of grace doesn't mean there is no personal cost to us once we are regenerated. Being one of God's children requires us to become what God has preordained us to be. And no matter what that predetermined purpose is, the warrior mentality will be part of it.

I know many young men who have yearned to make a difference in the world by joining military service. To become a sailor, marine, soldier, or airman, an oath must be taken. It goes as follows: "I do solemnly swear that I will support and defend the Constitution of the United States against all enemies, foreign and domestic; that I will bear true faith and allegiance to the same; and that I will obey the orders of the President of the United States and the orders of the officers appointed over me, according to regulations and the Uniform Code of Military Justice. So help me God."

That oath is just the beginning! Once the oath is taken the training begins to make the recruit into the image of a warrior. Months and even years are required for them to become ready and able to perform their sworn duties. The oath is followed by rigorous training beginning with boot camp. This beginning takes a young man or woman and breaks them down to their core. Once they are emptied of themselves the process of building them up to the services specifications begins. Only then can they be called a soldier, sailor, marine, or airman. And it is not over with boot camp. Many of these young men aspire to become elite. They want to be the best and serve among the best. For this to be achieved they must embrace an even more arduous training regime. This regime often includes schools and training that are hard to describe.

SERE School

SERE (Survival, Evasion, Resistance, and Escape) is actually an advanced code-of-conduct course. All military personnel get their initial code-of-conduct instruction during basic training in which they are taught an American service member's moral and legal responsibilities if captured by enemy forces. But SERE goes way beyond that. "We teach individuals what to do when things go from bad to worse," said Hospital Corpsman 1st Class Harry Haug, a SERE instructor assigned to Fleet Aviation Specialized Operational (FASO) training Group, Brunswick, Maine. The students who attend the course have a greater risk of being stranded behind enemy lines, said Haug. "They come here to learn how to stay alive and the values behind the code of conduct. When the situation is real, the threat is real, so these students need to be ready to handle it."

Aviators, force reconnaissance personnel, air crewmen, and Special Forces are the types of jobs that require SERE school training. While I was pastor in Coronado, California, I had the following sent to me by an elite Special Operator. He describes in detail just one evolution in the process required to equip him to handle the rigors of his chosen profession.

"I've spent the last two weeks going through the Navy's SERE school. Basically we learned how to live off the land (eating plants and bugs and stuff), then how to navigate around in the field, then how to resist if we're ever taken as a prisoner of war and finally how to escape if captured. During my experience I lost fifteen pounds and still haven't been able to put it back on! I look really thin around the face and neck and one could pretty much use me as a walking anatomy chart right now. The school sucked plain and simple! Because I was the senior ranking officer, or SRO, going through, I was responsible for the other students, all 24 men. So, I took much abuse from my 'captors.'

When we first got to the POW camp, they assigned us numbers to replace our names (to dehumanize us). I was kind of leery of how serious this school was going to be, because after all it was a SCHOOL! In a real POW situation, life would be a lot worse so I didn't know if I was going to be able to 'get into it' so to speak. When we got to the camp, they put canvas hoods over our heads and then lined us up to give us our numbers. Standing at attention in front of the Camp Major, who took my hood off, I was still thinking I was going to have trouble with getting into it.

The first thing the Camp Major said to me (screaming of course) was 'WHAT'S YOUR NAME CRIMINAL?' (Criminal referring to the fact that they looked at us as war criminals and not prisoners of war, another aspect of dehumanizing us). I replied 'Sir, (and then gave my name), sir!' No sooner had I finished saying those words, when from out of nowhere he reared back and decked me in the face, busting my nose open, which sent blood splashing across my face. I knew they had certain rules and restrictions that they had to follow and drawing blood was one that they weren't supposed to do. At that moment I thought to myself 'THIS GUY HAS MY COMPLETE AND UTTER ATTENTION!'

From then on I had no problem whatsoever with 'getting into it'! He gave me the war criminal number of 08. So from then on, I was referred to as War Criminal Zero-Eight, or just Zero-Eight. I then spent the next four or five hours in a brick cell a little smaller than the size of a bathtub with only my hood, a cup of water, and a pee/poop bucket. A lot of stuff happened after that, most of which involved me getting stomped, kicked, slapped, and thrown around the place. From the get-go I was getting beat not only for my own mistakes and such, but also for the other folks' (again, because I was the senior ranking officer).

"Sir... I, uh..." SMACK, STOMP, KICK! "I don't even know WHO XX is yet!!!" After hours of this kind of crud, it was VERY EASY for me to identify with Christ suffering for all of us! About 18 hours into this—way into the middle of the night—we were hauled out of our cells for 'work detail.' Oh yeah, did I mention that for the five days prior, none of us had eaten much more than a very small amount of flowers, bugs, and roots, nor had we gotten any sleep? Anyway, the guys were working and I was supposed to manage them. The work mostly entailed menial labor that had no point other than to wear us down. The head guard kept asking me every few minutes for a status of work progress. It took all I had to keep track of it all! Each time I fumbled with an answer...SMACK, STOMP, KICK! Or if one of the guys wasn't moving 'fast enough' or 'doing enough work'...SMACK, STOMP, KICK!

I was getting pretty worn out and my morale was terribly low. I spotted a campfire burning with a large pot on it. So, through the chilling cold that froze my bones stiff (because after a while, they stopped beating me and just started stripping my clothes off of me when someone messed up) and the delirium caused by lack of sleep, I shouted 'Sir, war criminal Zero-Eight respectfully requests that the criminals be given food and a little rest to enable them to increase work productivity, sir!' The head guard deliberated with the Camp Major who eventually told the head guard to feed us. They lined us up into two rows and sat us down. Producing a very large phone book-looking thing and in thickly Russian accented English, the head guard said, 'I know your disgusting American whore-dog customs. You make unheeded supplications to your God before you eat your meals. To show you how compassionate I am, I will allow one of you to do so now. Who would like to make this ridiculous gesture?'

Without hesitating, I shot to my feet and said, 'SIR, I WILL, SIR!!!' (Keep in mind here, that ALL of us were beat-down and our spirits were in the gutter.) 'Very well Zero-Eight...you have 10 seconds to decide what you want to say.' As I walked over to him,

I prayed in my head, 'God...You are everything. I am insufficient of myself. If You're ever going to make good on a promise to me, I beg that You do so now and give me the words I need!!!' When I got to where the head guard was standing, he handed me the phone book, which turned out to be a GIANT, coverless Bible! I took it from him and quickly started thumbing through the pages. Without so much as a thought of my own, I stopped on Psalm 91 and began reading....

I paused a moment to look up at my men. To the man, each of their eyes were filled with tears that were creating streaks of 'clean' down their dirty cheeks! Right then something like a truck slammed into me and knocked me to the ground. I landed on my face and my parched mouth filled with dirt as stars circled my head! The head guard then kicked me over, onto my back, grabbed me with both of his hands by the front of my shirt and lifted me to my feet (seemingly defying gravity and my body weight).

Then he started yanking me around, throwing me this way and that way all the while screaming at me from the top of his lungs. 'I AM YOUR MASTER!!! I CONTROL YOU...NOT YOUR GOD!!! WHERE IS HE NOW, YOU FILTHY AMERICAN WHORE-DOG!?!? YOU WILL SUBMIT TO ME!' He kept going and going and going. He must have tossed me around like a rag-doll for close to 10 minutes. But as soon as he said that he controlled me and not my God, a rush of excitement flooded through my body, numbing it completely against all the pain. I couldn't contain the joy I was feeling from this little brush with 'martyrdom!' The more he flung me about, the higher my spirits soared!

When he finished, he tossed me back toward my guys, who sat there awestruck! I sat up as erect as I could muster, wiped the blood, sweat, and tears from my face and just smiled my teeth off! The head guard then grabbed the Bible and shredded it into a dozen pieces, tossing them over the ground. At that moment I could have cared less if the world came to end! God had given me the words I needed when I needed them and moreover gave me the strength to endure persecution! Most importantly, He USED ME AS A TESTAMENT TO MY MEN!

Quite a number of the men afterward later admitted, 'Sir, I'm not a Christian, but when he ripped up that Bible, I really wanted to beat his ass!' Or 'Sir...I'm not a religious man, but God used your voice to speak to me last night!'"

The people running this SERE school and the students are all part of the same brotherhood. Those who run the camp are not putting the students through anything they themselves have not experienced. But they each accept the pain because it causes them to be prepared for any and all outcomes of war. Some may ask, why would a brother put another brother through such an experience? What possible benefit could come from such torture? The answer is competency. The realistic nature of the camp causes those who are subjected to its training to learn what cannot be taught from a book or manual. The SERE program takes its students to the end of themselves and causes each man to know himself for what he is, not what he thinks he is.

Have you ever read the passage that says, "iron sharpens iron?" Have you ever stopped to ask yourself what that means? It means resistance produces a sharpening which is synonymous with readiness. It means pressure from two equally strong elements causes both elements to be better. When was the last time you felt sharpened? Has there ever been a time you voluntarily submitted to an environment that caused you godly discomfort? Maybe it's time for you to seek such an environment.

God is not interested in making us comfortable. He wants us to be effective. Equipping is not comfortable. Some would say, "Why did God give us a comforter?" We have a Comforter because when we get after the job of enlarging the kingdom of God, things happen that cause us grief. It is then that we need the Comforter.

Crisis is a crucial crossroads in life. It is a turning point for better or worse. It is a time that calls for decisive action.

As Christians we believe that crisis does not cause decline but actually gives us a better understanding of what needs to change in order to be successful. Whether that crisis is in our personal life, our home, business, or even ministry, crisis reveals the cracks. It forces us out of complacency and mediocrity. Purification by crisis is designed by God to move us from one level of living to another, taking us to a greater experience of living the life we were all destined to live. It means to be like Christ, to live in such a way that we find a good death.

The cross for Jesus represented a crisis. It was a place of extreme torment in every conceivable way. But He was willing to endure that shame and embarrassment because in order to find a good death there was no other path for Him. "For the joy that was set before Him, He endured the cross..." (Hebrews 12:2).

Sacrifice is a part of the Christian life. Understand that you will only get out of this what you are willing to put into it. Accept the fact that pain is inevitable for victory to be achieved. Accept the call to eternal vigilance. Accept the fact that this is not about what YOU want. It is about what you can give through sacrifice to the success of the multitudes who make up the body of Christ..

CHAPTER 3

OPUS DEI

It was an early winter morning in the hills where we live outside of Nashville, Tennessee. We had just moved into our dream home a couple months earlier. It is a log home that was originally built during the Civil War, and for my wife and I, it is heaven on earth. With a 10-acre pasture between us and the two-lane frontage road and 33 acres of forest behind us, the silence makes for an awesome night's sleep. But on this particular date I tossed and turned all night. For no particular reason I could think of, sleep was fleeting.

Then, just before sunrise, when I was not completely awake, I began to repeatedly hear the words *Opus Dei*. Over and over again they came into my consciousness until I finally sat up in bed wide awake. From my studies I was aware that the words were Latin but like most of my college learning I had forgotten its complete meaning. So I stumbled into my office fumbling through my lexicons and looked up the term. Opus Dei means the work of God!

A look how the phrase was used in history revealed that during the Dark Ages the term was co-opted by a radical Catholic sect and was closely related to the famed Knights of the Templar. The sect was founded by a Jesuit priest who had some radical ideas more similar to extreme fundamentalist Christianity than Catholicism. In that they advocated such things as the separation between the genders except in marriage along with a form of scourging, or physically punishing one's self for sins.

After reading this, the obvious question for me was why would God speak those Latin words to me? Obviously the Dark Ages were not a good time for the Christian faith. It is called the "dark ages" because men misrepresented who God was in every conceivable way. Men calling themselves believers were doing atrocious things in the name of God. Murder of "infidels," torture of the innocent, and false doctrine were all pervasive practices in the Catholic Church during that time.

It stands to reason that something like self-punishment as a religious sign of holiness and other ridiculous functions in the attempts to please God were celebrated and even sought after because this was now deemed "holy"! Because "Christian" nations were led by royalty working alongside religiously zealous bishops and archbishops, royal leadership condoned the "law" that came from those who were supposed to hear God. So the people of faith suffered because of something that was supposed to bring them wholeness and peace.

When I "hear" something that I believe is from God it is my practice and responsibility to dismantle it to make sure it is truly from God. First I take what I have heard and test it by the Word of God to determine if it stands the test of Scripture. Once I feel that it does, my next test is to submit it to my peers and mentors to have them judge my conclusions. If it passes their test then I begin to chip away at all the man-made stuff surrounding what I have determined to be God in the attempt to dig out the true intended meaning.

God would not have spoken to me in Latin, a language I didn't speak or understand, unless He wanted me to know something of the original meaning of such a term. Also, God never speaks to someone unless what He says has an unfolding practical application to that day and hour. I quickly learned that the phrase was surrounded by religion, myth, and some truth. In the end, I came to the conclusion that God was wanting to redefine for this generation the meaning of the work of God, Opus Dei!

Today in many churches people are "tortured" with systems and programs that serve the vision of a local pastor but lack the larger plan of God. Parishioners are forced to think that the existing function of their church is exactly what Christ intended when He said, "I will build my church." They come to meet Jesus but statistics reveal that most leave feeling He is farther away than when they arrived.

In a study conducted by the Barna Group the following was revealed: Although many of the churchless hold positive views of churches, a substantial number also have no idea what Christians have accomplished in the nation, either for the better or for the worse. When the unchurched were asked to describe what they believe are the positive and negative contributions of Christianity in America, almost half (49%) could not identify a single favorable impact of the Christian community, while nearly two-fifths (37%) were unable to identify a negative impact.

Of those who could identify one way Christians contribute to the common good, the unchurched appreciate their influence when it comes to serving the poor and disadvantaged (22%), bolstering morals and values (10%), and helping people believe in God (8%). Among those who had a complaint about Christians in society, the unchurched were least favorably disposed toward violence in the name of Christ (18%), the church's stand against gay marriage (15%), sexual abuse scandals (13%), and involvement in politics (10%).

These statistics cannot be ignored. There is no way the downward spiral will stop in the church today unless the men who lead it are willing to look deep at what is lacking. This book is my attempt to underscore one of the areas missing, which is to fight evil in all it's forms, and enlist congregations in the fight that is a precursor to a good death. It is only upon that return to first principles that we will again see the power of God present in our midst with healing, miracles, and signs and wonders, revealing Jesus' pleasure with His church. This is Opus Dei!

Christ told the church in Luke 19:13 to "occupy till I come." The Greek word *occupy* means to be busy and to take possession. Occupy has one meaning to a soldier and another to a civilian. The civilian thinks of "occupying" as the process of making a place of comfort. When you say "occupy" to a soldier it carries the connotation of battle, blood, sweat, and tears. Because to occupy means to invade, extricate the enemy, and establish government.

It is clear that Scripture tells us that we all must act like soldiers: "Thou therefore endure hardness, as a good soldier of Jesus Christ. No man that wars entangles himself with the affairs of this life; that he may please him who hath chosen him to be a soldier" (2 Timothy 2:3-4).

As we see the fabric of our society unraveling and becoming more and more evil, we need to embrace the courage to admit that our present Christianity is not making the grade. Simply going to fellowship and praying with groups is not making things better. In fact I challenge the idea that prayer was ever supposed to be a singular focus among believers.

A "prayer movement" without a clarion call is not a movement at all. The most famous prayer meeting in the history of the church was attended by 120 believers. As they prayed, the Holy Spirit showed up and filled each of them with power. But it didn't stop there. The power was necessary for what they would be doing as a result of prayer. And the men and women who birthed the church departed that Upper Room directly into battle for the souls of mankind, to cast out demons, to heal the sick, and to raise the dead.

The results speak for themselves, as thousands were added to the church. And because they were brought into the kingdom of God by warriors, they emulated that spirit. The question for all church leaders today is simple. If we look at our systems, methods of church growth, and doctrines today, are they working as salt and light? Keeping people from the battle is not helping either them or the world.

Making our churches comfortable is not making the Comforter happy. Changing our doctrines to embrace sexual orientations God has clearly forbidden is an act of cowardice. Moving the lines of morality to bring in more people to our churches is the action of weak leadership. If as leaders we revere church growth more than the mission to overcome evil than we need to resign.

On occasion I am asked to address groups of new pastors and their wives. I consider it an honor to be among those who are willing to put their lives in ministry. They will become our leaders and those who set the standard for their city and new congregations. I prepare more for these meetings than almost any other because of what is at stake. When I went through seminary no one ever taught me about warfare. There was little if anything said about how ministry really is. I was taught how to exegete scripture and everything else about the business of ministry. There was a great deal said about the preparation of sermons, the activity that draws people and keeps them there. But I was never taught about the battle of planting a church.

Subsequently, when I did plant my first church I was hit between the eyes with the cost of my calling. The adjustment to reality took me time to make, but I made it. So when I address others who are about to plant a church, I give it to them the way I wish it would have been given to me. I ask, are you sure you want to do this? Because you will face conflict you never imagined. You may have the training to plant a church but when you arrive in your city and declare your intentions you have just entered your battlefield. I go on to say, if there is any quit in you, please just leave now and save yourself the trouble and discouragement of quitting. I continue by sharing personal stories of what my family endured as we pastored our churches. I speak vividly about the good and the bad because I want them to know that not only are they going to war but their families are as well. It is my belief that if I can talk them out of planting a church, then they are not ready or maybe not even called.

I have a dear friend who was the master chief of first phase BUD/S training for years. It was his duty to the SEAL community to weed out those who were not "SEAL material." First Phase, the basic conditioning phase, is seven weeks long and develops the class in physical training, water competency, and mental tenacity while continuing to build teamwork. Each week, the class is expected to do more running, swimming, and calisthenics than the week before, and each man's performance is measured by a four-mile timed run, a timed obstacle course, and a two-mile timed swim. In addition to physical training, the class also learns how to conduct hydrographic survey operations.

Because of its particularly challenging requirements, many candidates begin questioning their decision to come to BUD/S during First Phase, with a significant number deciding to Drop on Request (DOR). Historically, candidates who have composite Physical Screening Test (PST) scores below 800 are three times more likely to succeed than the average student. Most importantly, candidates who have made a full commitment to their goal of becoming a SEAL and those who decide ahead of time that quitting is not an option, regardless of how challenging the training becomes, dramatically increase their chances.

The fourth week of training is known as Hell Week. In this grueling five-and-a-half day stretch, each candidate sleeps only about four total hours but runs more than 200 miles and does physical training for more than 20 hours per day. Successful completion of Hell Week truly defines those candidates who have the commitment and dedication required of a SEAL. Hell Week is the ultimate test of a man's will and the class's teamwork. I once asked my friend, the Master Chief of First Phase, if he ever felt guilty when he convinced a BUD/S student to ring the bell three times. He sneered back at me and said the following: "Every SEAL before him had to face the same pressure but chose not to quit. It is my job to reveal what is really in each man. I am not there to babysit or show compassion because the battlefield is void of it."

When I see the large numbers of pastors who quit each year I have to ask, are we being honest with our pastor recruits when we convince them to enter ministry? Do we put them to the test? Are we really changing society for the better or are we becoming more like society? I think you know the answer. So, what are we going to do about it? I think the answer is, we need a mass presentation of men laying it all on the line before God, in a Romans 12:1-2 manner.

A Man Willing to Lay It All on the Line

The story of Nehemiah is amazing. In the 20th year of Artaxerxes, king of Persia (445/444 BCE), Nehemiah was cupbearer to the king. Upon learning that the remnant in Judah was in distress and that the walls of Jerusalem were broken down, he asked the king for permission to return and rebuild the city. Nehemiah was an important man. As the cupbearer of the king, his job status was at the top. In short, he had it made. Often as believers, our daily life is interrupted by the Holy Spirit. And when this happens, we begin to care about things we never thought we would concern ourselves with. When we accept the task associated with this interruption, what we had previously deemed important changes dramatically.

In Nehemiah's case, he was willing to place his posh position and job on the line because of what God was calling him to. When Jesus is Lord of your life, He alone has the right to change your direction. And while this may cause some discomfort, the fact that God trusts us with His will is the greatest of all honors for us. Nehemiah took the position in life to make a difference. For him, it was not enough just to have a great career and enjoy his life. He lived to make a difference. When he was made aware that the city of God, Jerusalem, was in shambles, he laid everything down and decided to change things.

Artaxerxes sent him to Judah as governor of the province with a mission to rebuild, letters explaining his support for the venture, and provision for timber from the king's forest. Once there, Nehemiah defied the opposition of Judah's enemies on all sides—Samaritans, Ammonites, Arabs, and Philistines—and rebuilt the walls within 52 days. Today it is typical for people to talk about what is wrong with the world. From politicians to bar patrons, that is where it stops, talk. But God is looking for men who are more action then talk. There is nothing more powerful than a man who lets his actions do the talking for him. Later, we will talk about the resistance which accompanies every act of courage, and how to deal with it.

Men, what message is your action communicating? When we understand that resistance is unavoidable when we follow God, a peace comes. But with that peace comes resolve and courage. Nehemiah was a man on fire. Once he decided to move, he would not be stopped. You see, there were people who not only were responsible for the destruction of Jerusalem, but they were bent on keeping it that way. They were happy with something grievous to God. So when a man showed up to deal with it, they chose to fight him thinking he would quickly retreat. That would not happen. Nehemiah had to make changes to his plan because of the resistance, but he took it in stride continuing the mission to restore. Real men on a real mission do not have a plan for defeat. The opposite is true. What Nehemiah shows us is that if we stay focused, God will meet us there, giving us the power and wisdom to succeed.

One of the great things I have learned during 30 years of serving God, is how great His favor is. Literally every time I have launched out to follow His leading, He met my move with favor and provision that has no natural explanation. And that is His promise. If we move in faith, He moves to make our path full of miracles. Nehemiah began his journey to follow God's leading in prayer. Nehemiah 1:4-5 says, "So it was, when I heard these words, that I sat down and wept, and mourned *for many days*; I was fasting and praying before the God of heaven. And I said: "I pray, Lord God of heaven, O great and awesome God...."

Preparation of our heart for God's mission cannot be overemphasized. We cannot just wing this. Nehemiah knew that his success was dependent upon the spirit of a man being fully led by the Holy Spirit. After Nehemiah prayed, he departed to do God's will not telling anyone about his mission. Upon arriving, people began to show up, presenting themselves as servants to him and his mission. When we are available to God, He makes sure others who are also available are drawn together like a magnet.

A New Discipleship

As leaders all of us are committed to making disciples. And we have produced many tools to help us reach that goal. The question is what kind of disciples are we making when those we've taught believe it a great accomplishment to learn foundational values of the Christian faith. Discipleship is simply ineffective if the message of discipleship does not include innovative thinking and integration into the battle of life. If we are making disciples after the Lamb of God; and not teaching also the spirit of the Lion of Judah then we are producing inept disciples.

Also, if our disciples believe that the heights of success are only found within the four walls of the church then we are doing society a great disservice. To truly set a disciple free to change the world, we must teach from experience, and that means as leaders we must have a revelation of mission-oriented Christianity. Christ came as a Lamb, He will come back as a Lion. He has promised us He will return, so the question is, what are we supposed to look like at that return? At that moment, we are to have His spirit, the spirit of a Lion.

So, what are we doing to produce lions? Are we as leaders creating examples others want to follow? While being a member in the church is an honorable role, being a fighter on the battlefield is where we are ultimately called. Being willing to lay our lives on the line for the sake of Christ means being willing to fight on the battlefield of business, the battlefield of politics, and the battlefield of culture.

There is a lack of courage demonstrated from our pulpits today. Our preachers are more interested in placating politicians and pacifying people than proclaiming the hard truth of the Bible. Trying to find a way to make our churches relevant has only served to make our churches inept. We do not exist to make men feel good about themselves at the expense of the truth. Regardless of the cost we are called by God to exemplify a standard which does not change on man's whim. While the majority of people today seek comfort and peace, is it possible that what they really need is pressure, the pressure of truth that liberates one by obliterating darkness?

When a man or woman decides to enter a police or military force they enter with one mindset, but exit completely transformed. This is because they have overcome the old self and completed every challenge needed to act in society with courage, in recognition of their duty. They are changed and unrecognizable compared to what they were. Is this not the definition of discipleship? Is this not the way to change the world we have been made stewards of?

As Matthew 28:18-20 declares, "Then Jesus came to them and said, 'All authority in heaven and on earth has been given to me. Therefore go and make disciples of all nations, baptizing them in the name of the Father and of the Son and of the Holy Spirit, and teaching them to obey everything I have commanded you. And surely I am with you always, to the very end of the age.'"

Every single one of Jesus' disciples died a good death. They put everything on the line for the sake of Christ. And since discipleship is the process of making disciples, then we should be the very example of what they exemplified. And as the "very end" comes closer, we should be as fierce as they were in the proclamation of our message, as fearless as they were in confronting evil, and filled with the belief of the giants of our faith.

CHAPTER 4

LIFE IN A WAR ZONE

For many years my family and I lived in San Diego, which is arguably one of the choice places in the United States to live and raise a family. The weather is great year round and there is little to complain about. The problem is there is so much to do there that only a fraction of people are interested in giving their Sundays or any other day to attend church. The ocean awaits along with a never-ending list of attractions, entertainment, and recreation. Church doesn't rank high on many priority lists. However, occasionally something happens to awaken the populace.

One such event occurred on a Sunday in late October of 2003 when the skies turned black at 2 o'clock in the afternoon. The dark shroud originated with the area's raging forest fires, then in their third day. As on any other Sunday, that morning we drove to church. En route to the school where our church met, we passed through Miramar Marine Base, engulfed by a rapidly moving blaze. A few minutes later we reached the spot where a man had just committed suicide by jumping off the bridge that links San Diego with Coronado Island. Later, as we attempted to drive home, a small plane crashed on a nearby freeway, closing many roads. Soon after, the "Amber Alert" announced a child kidnapping.

Understandably so, our children asked a load of questions that day. I seized the opportunity to earnestly discuss the eternal hope we have in Christ. I emphasized the need for all who follow Him to remain alert and avoid getting lulled into a passive faith. At one point I remarked, "This is what it must be like to live in a war zone." Suddenly, it seemed as if time stood still. I sensed God saying softly, "You do live in a war zone."

I have come to the conclusion that war, whether it is natural or spiritual, causes men to conduct their lives vastly different from those who refuse to engage in it. Before I go too much further, let me make one thing clear. I am not a warmonger who has some sort of morbid fascination with death and destruction. God knows I have been accused of it since I have spent more than a decade working with those who serve this and other nations in military and law enforcement service. I hate war! The more I see of it the more I disdain it. I not only see the toll it has on those unfortunate enough to experience war in their land but also the toll it has on those who are called to fight it along with their families. There is nothing about war that pleases God. The fact is, wars are here to stay and until Jesus comes to redeem the world from the hold Satan has on it, we will have to accept that dark reality.

Jesus Himself said in Matthew 24:6, *"You will hear of wars and rumors of wars, but see to it that you are not alarmed. Such things must happen, but the end is still to come."* Wars and battles are the unfortunate byproduct of a fallen world! When men are stirred by the demonic hosts who celebrate death and destruction, war is the result. I am sure that such thoughts cause many to turn away and many reading this will want to do what others over the centuries have done and seek some place where war doesn't intrude. There are monasteries where monks hang out meditating and ignoring the rest of the world in seeming peace. There are religions that preach the panacea that we are promised a place on earth that is free from all conflict and war. There is a growing sentiment in secular society which preaches pacifism as the best reaction to evil. These pacifists condemn any confrontation with evil. They believe that it is possible for men to all get along. This is no new argument. Men have been arguing back and forth for centuries about the possibility that pacifism could rule society. Figures like Henry David Thoreau, Mahatma Gandhi, and Martin Luther King, Jr. are cited as examples. While these individuals were clearly admirable, the case can be made that in their attempts to be true to their consciences they only incited the very thing they abhorred.

"It is argued that pacifism possesses a sublime arrogance in its implicit assumption that its adherence allows one to dictate the terms of struggle in any conflict with the state. The example of the Jews under Nazism reveals the basic illogical assumptions embedded at the very core of pacifist conceptions of morality and political action. Pacifism assumes the configuration of a pathological illness when advanced as a political methodology; as such, pacifism is delusional, racist, and suicidal. Given its deep-seated, superficially self-serving, and socially approved nature, pacifism is likely to be difficult to treat and is a long-term barrier to the formation of revolutionary consciousness/action in the US." (PsycINFO Database Record (c) 2012 APA, all rights reserved) http://psycnet.apa.org/psycinfo/1987-15425-001).

War preceded man in creation. The battle in the heavens is clearly outlined in Scripture. As Luke 10:18 states, "And He said to them, 'I saw Satan fall like lightning from heaven.'" War between Christ and Satan will unveil the end of mankind as it is revealed in Revelations 1:19, "Then the fifth angel sounded, and I saw a star from heaven which had fallen to the earth; and the key of the bottomless pit was given to him."

The battles we are born into, whether natural or spiritual, will always be with us. To embrace that fact will change the way we live our lives. A man who knows he is at war lives soberly, on alert, and training is always part of his life. Most Christians would likely agree that we live in the midst of a spiritual war. But that fact is not just something in the ethereal and unseen. Evil spiritual activity initiates a natural evil partner. All natural evil finds its beginning in the spiritual.

Warfare will be with us as long as man lives on this earth—or at least until Christ returns. Because of the nature of humanity, we can never relax and enjoy an era without conflict, whether that be a natural one or a spiritual one or both. The time for peace is in our eternal existence in God's presence. That was true for Jesus and it will be true for us. We have an adversary! He is formidable and fortified and will be here until Jesus Himself comes to the earth and deals with him once and for all.

Wasted Faith

What if I were to tell you that the United States military strategy for drawing soldiers is to provide an environment of ease and lack of pressure. What kind of troops do you think we would draw? It would draw a people who think that someone owes them something. It would draw a people who are more interested in what they can get out of the military than what they can add to it. It would draw a people who would complain about training and run for the hills when the war comes.

We need to stop spiritualizing things as an escape and get down and dirty to deal with this cancer that is stealing our callings. I have to wonder if the rise in the levels of serious depression among believers is not really the prodding of the Holy Spirit accentuating the absence of a fundamental facet of faith, the warrior heart. Think about it, when you are fighting a battle you don't have time to obsess about yourself. You are focused and alert and there is a sobriety that comes over you to keep a vigil and when you encounter the enemy you are more then ready to face him. Depression has no place in a man engaged!

Abraham Lincoln warned, "You can't escape the responsibility of tomorrow by evading it today."[1] Evasion stems from weakness and has no place in Christendom. Sound heartless? Since we are called "Christians," we are *duty bound* to live our lives in such a way that Christ is exemplified through our actions. Christ never evaded anything! He spent His life pursuing victory over the forces of darkness and stopped at nothing to obtain it until He finished the fight. As a result, He gained victory for all people. I think we live in a time of transition where Christ is about to reveal a new leadership along with ideas filled with His wisdom. This book is written to stimulate a sense of inner crisis among all who hunger for something that is clearly not from ego or hype.

I admire such leaders as the late Harry S. Truman. That great president noted, "Men make history, and not the other way around. In periods where there is no leadership, society stands still. Progress occurs when courageous, skillful leaders seize the opportunity to change things for the better." In a revealing interview with Drew University's Darrell Cole, *Christianity Today* asked the professor of religion why our society has the impression that most early Christians were pacifists. His response was striking: "We've gotten that idea because many scholars early in the 19th century were basing their research on incomplete data. Those researchers were generally very much liberal humanists. They wanted to see Jesus, Jesus' followers, and the early church in their own way of life. Research over the past 50 or 60 years has shown that the term pacifism, as we use it to mean that all bloodshed is inherently evil—simply did not exist in the early Christian community. Early Christians did not participate in war because the Roman soldiers distrusted them and because to be a Roman soldier you had to participate in pagan rites. When those two things fell apart, Christians started joining in droves. So by the time you get to Constantine, in the early 4th century, you've got whole Christian battalions." Wow!

Before leaving office, Minnesota Governor Jesse Ventura, who also served as a Navy SEAL, publicly stated that religion is for weak people. The governor was well-known for spouting brash opinions, but this time I took special notice. Many of my colleagues made statements such as, "How dare he speak of our faith in that manner?" or "Who does he think he is?" However, I recognized that many special operators share his opinion. Many in the faith community condemned Ventura, but to me his comment deserves a respectful evaluation.

Contrary to the governor's statement, Scripture reveals a faith that produces the strong, not the weak. The Bible contains hundreds of examples of courageous, strong, and valiant men and women who risked their lives for the good of others. So why are Christ's followers today perceived as weak? Could it be that the former governor's comment represents an indictment of the modern church?

While the twenty-first century church should demonstrate biblical heroism, instead it exhibits timidity and moral weakness. It is understandable that few soldiers want to follow a faith whose stories of courage, faith, and sacrifice exist in the past. For too long this grave discrepancy has been a deterrent to men and women who have a calling and desire to serve God as warriors.

Perhaps church leadership is mostly to blame for this soft image. Demographer George Barna says that more than 1,600 pastors a month leave the pulpit due to depression. At first glance I felt sympathetic toward these people, wondering what devastating events drove them to abandon their calling. Then my sorrow turned to anger when I realized I couldn't think of a single week when something depressing hadn't occurred in my career. That led me to ask: Why are we putting those who cannot handle the harsh realities of the battle of ministry in leadership? No matter what happens, we must never abandon our position. Never! That is the example of Christ and those who birthed the first century church. It should be the example of all who lead today.

One must wonder what values seminaries are teaching when so many ministers leave their pulpits because they are depressed! I may sound harsh, but if a minister abandons his post because the job wasn't what he envisioned, I question his fitness to lead to begin with. The last thing the church needs is a spineless leader.

Experience has taught me ministry is a war zone! A pastor is supposed to have more than a mindset to draw people into his congregation. Pastors are supposed to continually fight for their cities, their people, and their God-given mandate. They are supposed to train strong disciples fending off the demons that resist the advance of a warrior's commitment.

"The only easy day was yesterday!" This is the SEAL motto which every person on the post has to read when entering the doors of the compound that forges America's elite Naval warriors. This motto should be the same for every Bible college and seminary in the world today. If we as church leaders live by that code, no one would dare call our faith weak.

I am not saying that there is not a place for gentleness, peace, and kindness. These are qualities that stem from a Spirit-filled life and are prized values in Christian relationships. In relationship to the evil of this world, both in natural and spiritual warfare, Christ teaches His children to recognize that they are called to battle. The idea that believers should be nice and passive concerning evil is not scriptural.

When the Bible exhorts us to turn the other cheek or pray for those who persecute us, these actions are only a sign of submission to the Lord to direct our response to the attack. It is a sign of submission to our Head and the Lord of the fight. It is not a call for passivity when evil raises its head against us. The key is to allow the Lord to institute a strategy to defeat those bent on our demise. We are called to love our enemies but loving our enemies and being nice to them while they pummel us is another thing altogether. Let's face it, Jesus wasn't nice one single time when facing evil and He didn't tell us to be nice to it either His return will not be marked with niceties as He arrives to pummel Satan and all his imps.

As award-winning writer Philip Yancey asks, "How would telling people to be nice to one another get a man crucified? What government would execute Mister Rogers or Captain Kangaroo?"[5] When soldiers respond to an attack by our nation's enemies, we don't want them to turn the other cheek. We want them to return lethal fire. When an intruder invades our home, we don't want the authorities to gently persuade them to leave. We want them to forcefully remove the threat to our loved ones. It is no different with spiritual warfare and the invading forces that seek to destroy our homes, marriages, children, and faith.

The church must embrace the spirit of the Lion of Zion and the returning King. In this post 9-11 world, the church will either make that change or it will risk being overrun by godless religions and Third World despots. The 9-11 terrorist attacks were a message to believers everywhere to receive the spirit of a lion. We need to take on that nature!

I say this because there are too many quitters in the church today. According to Scripture the problem is not going to get better but worse. Paul gave an ominous prediction of the state of Christendom previous to the coming of Christ in 2 Thessalonians 2:3, "Let no man beguile you in any wise: for *it will not be*, except the falling away come first, and the man of sin be revealed, the son of perdition." If we are not motivated to shore up the heart of the church at that, we are already in serious trouble.

I don't think the term "Christian" was ever intended to be understood devoid of the identification with a military character. One of the reasons for the lack of a warrior spirit in the church is due partly to the lack of involvement the church has had in recent years with the warrior. While searching for information on the last time the church was involved to any large extent with the military, I was surprised to find that it was during the Civil War.

Since then, military life and lives have fallen into somewhat of a void in the vision of most churches. Due to the vagabond nature of the typical military life most churches have a hard time considering ministry to them because their presence is so off and on. The typical stay in a city for someone in military service is two years. Unfortunately, their absence among us in our churches has not only left a void, but the centurion's faith is kept from us.

I remember one Sunday I arrived at church and noticed a man sitting in the back with a bandage on his neck. A closer look revealed a dear friend who had been gone for some time with his SEAL team. When I asked him what happened to his neck he replied smugly, "Oh, just a stray bullet, no big deal!"

What would we be like if every Christian embraced the attitude of a warrior, one who NEVER retires? What would we be if we integrated that mindset into our present perspective? When you think about it, many believers today have lost the passion to serve Christ. Notice I said passion! It isn't that they have lost the desire to remain faithful, read their Bible, and follow its message, it's just that the passion is gone. I was one of those believers, and the worst part of all is, as a pastor, I was supposed to be setting the standard for excellence in Christian character.

Passion is an interesting thing. It is a gift to us as long as we are where God wants us. When we are out of the will of God, passion seeks a fulfillment that can ruin a man. It is clear to me that one quality seen in every man or woman of God who finished the fight of life is the fact that they stayed engaged in the battle until they breathed their last breath. It is also clear to me that there is significant evidence that those who "retired" from the fight have proven the folly of such a decision.

CHAPTER 5

WHEN KINGS GO TO WAR

Studying history is one of my favorite pastimes. That is why I love the Bible so much. I become easily engrossed in Old Testament writings, especially those that tell of how God, in spite of their obvious weaknesses, used men to do great things. For thousands of years many of these men stood out as examples, leaving us black and white principles to guide our lives.

David was a warrior before he was a ruler! The thing God used most to qualify him to be a ruler was the test of battle. He began to learn courage and responsibility outside the view of men. David wasn't interested in what others thought of him or in the applause of men. He was interested in what God thought of him. Being a good steward of his sheep was what David expected of himself. He practiced with his sling day after day because the possibility of animal attacks was always possible. Because of his self-training, when a lion or bear did show up, David killed them.

Character doesn't just show up one day out of the blue. It is the result of discipline and training. It was that kind of attitude that made David respond so viscerally when he heard that a giant was taunting the great armies of Israel. David couldn't believe that his brothers, the army, and its king, were rendered inept due to the taunting of a Goliath. For David, who was used to fighting "impossible" enemies, such behavior demanded confrontation. God used these battles both to test the character and passion of this future king, but also to reveal him.

David's unwillingness to give any ground to the enemy caused God to label him with an enviable title, "a man after God's own heart!" Doesn't that speak volumes? God is saying that the heart of the Godhead is to give no ground to the enemy. Not one inch! If we are to follow in the footsteps of David and become men after God's own heart then we must have the same attitude concerning the ground between the enemy and us.

David was certainly not perfect and we have much to learn from what he revealed in his time of weakness. The king, after fighting many battles for God, decided to remain home in the comfort of his palace while his subordinate, Joab, went to lead the battle in his stead. I can understand David's actions, as I am sure he felt that he deserved a break from the battlefield. He likely came to the conclusion that staying home for this one battle was completely acceptable and he had earned a vacation from it all. David watched as his army marched off to the battle until they were out of sight. I would think that somewhere down in his gut there was a sick feeling.

Because David knew in his heart that he was not where he was destined to be, the passion for fighting God's wars must have begun to steal his sleep. One night he was so distressed that he went out on his balcony to walk. While walking and thinking, he was stricken with the sight of a young woman bathing on her roof. This difficult moment in the king's life communicates a stark message. If you are not in the war you're called to, you will be in a war you're not called to. There is no more dangerous man than one who is NOT where he is supposed to be and NOT doing what he has been called by God to do. If David were where he was supposed to be, with his troops, there would be one less chapter in the Bible, the chapter about a king who didn't go to war.

Passion without holy expression is dangerous and can be life altering. Today there is an epidemic among Christians regarding lust and pornography. A 1996 Promise Keepers survey at one of their stadium events revealed that more than 50% of the men in attendance were involved with pornography within one week of attending the event. Fifty-one percent of pastors say cyber-porn is a possible temptation and 37% say it is a current struggle (*Christianity Today*, Leadership Survey, 12/2001). More than half of evangelical pastors admit viewing pornography last year.

Roger Charman of Focus on the Family's Pastoral Ministries reports that approximately 20 percent of the calls received on their Pastoral Care Line are for help with issues such as pornography and compulsive sexual behavior. In a 2000 *Christianity Today* survey, 33% of clergy admitted to having visited a sexually explicit Web site. Of those who had visited a porn site, 53% had visited such sites "a few times" in the past year, and 18% visit sexually explicit sites between a couple of times a month and more than once a week. Twenty-nine percent of born again adults in the U.S. feel it is morally acceptable to view movies with explicit sexual behavior, according to The Barna Group.

Fifty-seven percent of pastors say that addiction to pornography is the most sexually damaging issue to their congregation (*Leadership Journal* Survey, March 2005). Seventy percent of American men ages 18–34 view Internet pornography once a month. This shocking fact is one of many that *Christianity Today* consulting editor John W. Kennedy found during his research for the magazine's cover story, "Help for the Sexually Desperate."

And don't assume that porn isn't a problem in your church. One evangelical leader was skeptical of survey findings that said 50 percent of Christian men have looked at porn recently. So he surveyed his own congregation. He found that 60 percent had done so within the past year, and 25 percent within the past 30 days. Other surveys reveal that one in three visitors to adult websites are women. Porn is gaining a stranglehold on mainstream American culture.

One reason is the false message that porn viewing is harmless and socially acceptable for the sexually frustrated. One reason it is not harmless is the number of casual porn viewers who end up sexually addicted. The term sexual addiction is only 25 years old. But it describes the very real problem of extreme sexual behavior that is destructive to self and others. In his research, John W. Kennedy found that experts believe tens of millions of people are addicted to sex.

Stigma and fear work against Christians who wish to address this issue in the community of their church. Kennedy himself bears witness to this reality. He became motivated to write about sex addiction after his pastor stonewalled his request to start a confidential men's accountability group. The pastor basically said the issue was too hot to handle. After much prayer, John decided to change churches and then contacted *Christianity Today* to begin writing the article.

John's thorough reporting grants church leaders an unprecedented look into the way men's accountability groups function. One crucial element is creating a confidential context for full disclosure. John said, "I'm a guy. And just about everybody has struggled with this at one time or another. But we don't talk about that at church usually." Disclosure of sex addiction or porn use is so stigmatizing that it is best handled in a confidential, small-group setting in which participants agree not to pass judgment. They also grant each other "the right to call" 24/7 for unannounced check-ins.

"The thing that struck me the most in talking with these men is that I found an honesty rarely apparent in the church," John told me. "These guys are real. They are transparent, honest, no bull, no plastic smiles." Some of John's recommendations for starting a men's accountability group include starting small, extending the group's focus beyond sexuality only, and maintaining its Christian purpose. This reminds me of how distinctive Christian community is.

"Because Christian community is founded solely on Jesus Christ, it is a spiritual and not a psychic reality. In this, it differs absolutely from all other communities," said Dietrich Bonhoeffer, perfectly summing up what faithful, risk-taking congregations offer a sexually obsessed society.

David's tragedy teaches us some interesting truths. First, when we are not where we are supposed to be, we are not equipped to deal with the temptations that come. I am not just referring to a geographical place but a mindset. Second, when our passion is not focused on what God has called us to we will try to quench it through life-ruining means and finally, when we are out of the will of God we write chapters in the story of our lives God never wanted written.

The character of a warrior is something Christ never intended the believer to lose. He wanted His people to always have within them the heart to fight. Most of the Bible speaks about times of war. Warfare is a theme that is unavoidable from beginning to end and those who were fighting it were God-anointed people. It is true that we are promised times or seasons of peace but that will not be in this lifetime. So then, what does it mean to put on the full amour of God? I don't mean some imaginary act that we live out each day but what does it REALLY mean? Can a believer actually be an "anointed warrior?"

I was once invited to appear on a live television broadcast to speak about some of the things God is doing through FORCE Ministries. Appearing with me was a Navy SEAL and before the broadcast, I tried to get an idea of what kind of questions would be asked so we could be prepared to give concise answers. I soon realized that the format of the show was more of a shoot from the hip thing. The host was a nice man who picked us up at the hotel and drove us to the show. While driving we expected him to set up the show but instead we only shot the breeze and heard of the hosts exploits and accomplishments. He was a "veteran" TV personality and we figured that he would know best how to couch things so to gain the best effect.

So the show began and we were introduced. As it should be, the SEAL was the highlight of the show and the show focused for some time on his military activities. Then it happened! The host began to state his opinion about war and while we listened he made several comments about the need for us to get out of the war in the Persian Gulf. He stated that we needed to do everything in our power to stop our activities and get home. After a few awkward moments of silence I said, God has anointed men and women for the purpose of fighting wars. These anointed people need to be where they are until the enemy either surrenders or is eliminated. Then I pointed to the Navy SEAL next to me and said, "This man and others like him are God's agents of destruction to tyrants, despots, and evil men throughout the world. When, and only when, victory is achieved, which means the elimination or surrender of these people, should our people come home."

My host that day most likely didn't like what I said but it still needed to be said. Unfortunately, too many people think that whacking a few bad guys wins a war. The truth of the matter is there will always be demonic activity and bad guys. This means that there will always be plenty of places for war to be fought. It is an "HONORABLE" thing to be God's agent of destruction to these despots. When asked if those who planned the 9/11 attack on the Twin Towers should be forgiven, General Tommy Franks responded: "Only God can forgive such people and I am here to arrange the meeting!"

Satan is an enemy who cannot be rehabilitated! He has one agenda, to take as many human agents to hell with him as possible. He is the ultimate terrorist! No matter how innocent or pure the victim, he wants to bring destruction to them. There is only one element on earth to arrest his activities, Christian people who are in the battle for the long haul. I'm talking about intercessors, prayer warriors, preachers, teachers, and "normal people" who refuse to be intimidated by the enemy. These are people who are prepared to be attacked and know that at times it will hurt to be a warrior but are determined to stay in the battle until the Lord comes back.

Working with today's natural warriors has taught me some valuable lessons. Most of those lessons have come by way of observations I have made in watching them deal with human emotion. By the way, these are the same emotions that everybody else deals with. What distinguishes a soldier from a civilian is in the dealing with the emotion. You see, a soldier is enlisted or volunteers into the service of something greater than himself. He is duty bound to uphold a commitment made before he entered military service. That means that DUTY holds more value than any (yes I said any) emotion.

Translated, that means that no matter how a soldier feels, he WILL complete his task regardless of the cost. I often receive letters and e-mails from people who are serving in harm's way in the service of this country. I have to admit that some of them are difficult to read because in their reading one can easily see the struggle of the heart. Once such letter came from a "special operator" serving in the Middle East. He wrote:

"PG, (they called me PG, which stands for Pastor Greg) It's really hard, man. I hate to call you "man" but I want to talk to you like you're one of the guys. It's difficult being in this position. I am always thinking of God's will and I'm not sure of His intentions. What I mean is that when we are doing our job, it isn't pretty. We are not here to win the hearts and minds of the local people like the conventional forces are here to do. We do some ugly stuff but it's only to keep us from being the prey. We always have to be the predators over here and it seems OK just as long as you don't dwell on it. After we do a job, the guys shrug it off as no big deal but the truth of the matter is that it is a very big deal. We go after the baddest dudes on the block and so far we have been successful. However, I do wonder how God sees it. We are getting some, and going all the way. It's an adrenaline rush that I can't compare to anything. Afterward, you get drained and have gnarly dreams. Life is so cheap here. It's no wonder that they are so willing to be suicide bombers. They have nothing to live for. What sucks is the statistic that the average death rate here is 1 US soldier per day. They are following their belief of "death by a thousand cuts." Out of 125,000 that sounds pretty good but lately we have been close to making the average go up. Look, the bottom line is this...when I first got here I prayed all the time that we would not get hurt and now I'm like, "If it's time then it's time." I know God is watching over me but I haven't heard much from Him. So I am chugging along like I always have. I'm trying to do the right things. There isn't much sin to be had here with the exceptions of my emotions. I can't stomach this country or the people in it. I try to realize that not all of them are bad but it's hard when you know the truth about this place. It's evil and there is no way around it."

Now that you have read this once, try reading it again! Now this time look not so much at what is said, but at what is not said. This man is called to do something horrendous. During his duties he is required to take a human life. In the process of fulfilling his duties there is a great human cost on both ends of the gun sight. The things he is seeing and has seen will never be gone from his memory. Nightmares, dreams, and memories will be forever a part of his existence. So what is he supposed to do? Should he leave his battleground, should he tell his command that the stress is too much for him. Should he be a victim? NO! He just needs to DEAL WITH IT and keep fighting. WOW! Isn't that offensive? Isn't that obnoxious? No, that is what life is like in a war zone. You say, "OK, but I don't live in a war zone." I am sorry to give you the news but yes you do!

I am always struck with the story of Elijah and his response to the attack of Jezebel. Here is this unbelievable warrior who is threatened by Jezebel and he does something completely unlike him; he runs out into the desert and hides under a "broom tree." While sitting there he begins to wish he was dead and moans his very existence. As you can imagine God is watching all this and He let it go until He was fed up with it. I love the reaction of God to His man's cowardly actions. He asked, "Elijah, what are you doing here?"

Elijah began by reiterating all the reasons he was there and again God's response is striking. "GET UP!" If I were to put it into today's vernacular I would say it this way: Get up, quit whining, and get back into the battle. In other words, get up, quit being a victim, and get back to the calling I have placed upon you. You see, while Elijah was sitting under the broom tree feeling sorry for himself he was MISREPRESENTING the God he was supposed to be representing. For God, that was UNACCEPTABLE!

I don't think God is very happy today with the many excuses men make to somehow excuse them from battle. We are adept at coming up with excuses based on all our bad experiences and we somehow think God will understand. If God were to show up today and confront much of His church I wonder how many of us would hear the same words as Elijah?

Today we aren't taught to just deal with things. It seems that in this world the popular notion is there are really two categories of people. There are the "victims" and there are the "victimizers." Today it seems that if you are a leader, you most likely will be made out to be a "victimizer." It seems that if you are someone who just deals with things and stays in the battle you are made out to be the bad guy. The truth is society seems to make life easier for the victim. If you have an addiction, bigotry, a perversion, or any other type of bondage it must be someone else's fault. If it didn't happen out of the womb then it must have happened when you were in the womb, but your problem means you are a victim. If you are a victim then everyone else owes you something.

As a victim you can walk around with your hand out and your face down and get by in life fairly well. You won't have to fight any battles, face any pressure, or stretch yourself beyond your desires. What is interesting is that many of these victims attend churches where they are made to believe that it is OK to carry on life like this. I hate to say it but theologically God gives no place to such thinking. Whatever happened to "go and sin no more"? Whatever happened to "forgive and you will be forgiven"?

In the first chapter of Jeremiah there is a great story of a would-be prophet who is attempting to change God's mind about his calling. Jeremiah 1:4-6 says, "Then the word of the LORD came unto me, saying, Before I formed you in the belly I knew you; and before you came forth out of the womb I sanctified you, and I ordained you a prophet unto the nations. Then said I, Ah, Lord GOD! Behold, I cannot speak: for I am a child."

Jeremiah was a man with emotional strengths and weaknesses just like the rest of us. One of his weaknesses seems to be that he was afraid of people. I think the psychological term for it is agoraphobia! The word agoraphobia is derived from Greek words literally meaning "fear of the marketplace." The term is used to describe an irrational and often disabling fear of being out in public. Look at this from Jeremiah's perspective.

Here God is calling him to be a PROPHET. Prophets are people who speak to large crowds and great leaders. Among other things they are people who confront, judge, and pronounce unpopular messages. On occasion they are people who even have to physically act out messages. To a schooled actor that would be a great thing, but to the agoraphobic?

So Jeremiah understandably attempts to talk God out of it. Again, what is interesting to me is God's response. "Say not, I am a child: for you shall go to all that I shall send you, and whatsoever I command you thou shalt speak." God didn't sit with Jeremiah and cry with him or change His mind about his calling. Instead, God in essence said, GET OVER IT! You will do what I have called you to and furthermore you will do it exactly the way I tell you to.

Ahhhhh, that's not very nice of God. He sure doesn't seem very sensitive! Maybe not but He does seem militaristic. You see the call of God is not an invitation. It is an order! We will all be judged in eternity on what we did with the talents we were given. To stand before God and say that we didn't respond to His call because we were AFRAID? Well, let's just say I don't think we will get too far!

FEAR IS SOMETHING TO BE FACED AND OVERCOME! It is not something that is supposed to rule your life and existence. Many believers ACCEPT their fear and think God accepts it too. That's called delusional! If God refuses to accept our fears then we need to do the same. What is it about the church that we are so afraid to challenge one another? Why is it that the sports community, the military world, the corporate world, and the political world thrive on challenging one another but somehow in the church we are supposed to remain neutral?

As a federal chaplain I have had the pleasure of working with a number of military chaplains. I have found most of them to be a unique people who have a heart to really make a difference in the men and women who serve this nation. But I was deeply disturbed when I learned that part of the responsibility of a chaplain is to maintain a neutral position on religious matters and make a decision not to proselytize.

Now I don't want to in any way disparage the image of the chaplain but many, if not all the chaplains I have met, have divulged to me that there is a morale problem in the chaplaincy. It is no wonder! What man with a true conviction in his heart wants to spend the majority of his time presiding over either a ceremony or a funeral? Where is the place for conviction?

In a world where men and women are called to give their lives in battle and would willingly do so if required because of a deep heart felt conviction why would we expect the chaplain to be respected when they are asked to keep their conviction, under wraps? When conviction is not given an expression morale goes out the window. As Revelation 12:11 says, "And they overcame him by the blood of the Lamb, and by the word of their testimony; and they loved not their lives unto the death."

I once had a friend tell me that he walked on hot coals to demonstrate confidence. After further discussion, I found that he was attending a positive thinking seminar conducted by a popular seminar speaker. I must admit that my first reaction was not all that good. But when I thought about it more deeply, I realized that this seminar was successful solely because it helped people overcome once single enemy, fear! Disclaimer: I am not advocating walking on hot coals. I think there are many better ways to gain confidence.

Wherever fear is required to be faced and overcome, the result is a better man! One obvious illustration of this is the United States military! Each soldier, marine, airman, or sailor is required to go through boot camp. While I'm sure each member of their particular branch of service thinks his boot camp is the most arduous, all of them have something in common: a process of breaking men down and then rebuilding them.

In boot camp, fears are overcome on a daily basis. Each man has no choice but to overcome because in war there is no room for fear when it stands in the way of fulfilling the mission. This is not to say that these men and women are completely absent of fears after boot camp. However, they are taught that fear is not an excuse to not act. They are taught to overcome in the moment, deal with the emotion, and do what the mission requires. That is what makes the strongest military on earth!

I recently saw a post on Facebook where a pastor is standing on stage holding a large sword. He told his congregants that he was a warrior and intended to use the sword to "do business." The problem is, he was about completely out of shape, and clearly didn't know the first thing about how to hold a sword, or for that matter how he would use it in conflict. I was tempted to reply, "Slowly put the sword down before you hurt yourself."

That is exactly the way I see many Christians today. We try to act the act, but we have not yet disciplined ourselves to do what Christ told us to do. We are overcoming because we practice overcoming. I guarantee you, once you begin to face your fears you will become a transformed man. You will become the man God created you to be, a warrior for Christ!

"When your time comes to die, be not like those whose hearts are filled with fear of death, so that when their times comes they weep and pray for a little more time to live their lives over again in a different way. Sing your death song, and die like a hero going home."

Tecumseh

CHAPTER 6

BLURRY VISION

*"The underlying apologetic for all of theology
is spiritual warfare."*

John Bishop

Through most of my life I was left to figure most things out for myself. Since my mother died at a young age my father was unengaged, I was used to that kind of life and it never occurred to me that this kind of thing is unnatural. As a first generation Christian I would watch how things were done in the church and copy the pattern. When it was time for me to move out into my own calling I took all the things I saw my pastor do and copied them into what I was doing.

I can tell you that among the top things I was taught was the importance of having and following a vision. For me life void of vision was the same as death. I was never taught anything different! It was expected of someone in my position—cast the vision, hold people to it, and move methodically until you reach it. Once you are there, come up with another vision, and so on. In my world, either you had a vision or you were following someone who did. Now I think that premise is somewhat flawed and has contributed to the loss of too many potentially great warriors.

Vision is the result of a God-given word establishing a mandate for action. But it doesn't stop there! Vision is a complicated issue because it is not only important to know what God wants you to do but also what is involved in the building of a vision. I like to say its rise is similar to the rise of a building or structure. The foundation is laid wide and should take the most time because it will hold up all that will rise from it. Sometimes, in our zeal to build, we spend way too little time on the foundation, which can have cataclysmic consequences in the future.

A vision that is destined to succeed is one that is built upon a foundation of prayerful thought, along with godly counsel, which results in a structure that reflects God's ownership. When this method is the process of a vision's stewards, then what is built will become a fortification against all attacks of the enemy. Also, a vision that destined to succeed is one that is built upon a foundation of sound theological principles. This includes a commitment to the protection of truth and involves a plan for church-wide spiritual and sometimes natural battle. The implementation of vision cannot be seen as anything other than the declaration of war on evil. If a man dares to think otherwise he is a fool and will soon be proven wrong. It is important then to understand vision and the process it follows over time and implementation.

The Evolution of Vision

The evolution of vision involves the battle from visionary to dreamer. There is a reason why Scripture tell us "your old men shall dream dreams, and your young men shall see visions." God wanted men to know that there is a transition for all men that will be determined by age and experience. He wanted men to know that the path of vision is for the young men and that at some point every visionary will have to face the transition from the life of a visionary to that of a dreamer. If the visionary doesn't expect this transition, then the possibility exists that he will fall into the same shameful trap men have fallen into for thousands of years. Time is too short to allow this to continue!

Having made that transition I can tell you from personal experience I was not ready for it. No one ever told me that this was ahead for me. As a result, when I entered the void between visions and dreams I faced the greatest temptation of my life to quit. I felt that God had abandoned me, that I had failed Him, that my ministry was being judged and found to be a failure. While none of this was true, I nonetheless convinced my soul it was. Looking back, if someone had modeled the navigation of this transition for me, giving me a pattern to draw from, I am sure I would have walked through the void better. In my communication with leaders today, young and old, I have determined that most of them don't even realize that this process even exists.

One conversation I had with a young pastor underscored this contention. He was vibrant and full of God. He had all the bells and whistles of a potentially successful minister. The young man had it all down regarding what was needed to build a great church. His attitude was bolstered due to the huge successes he was seeing in his recent church plant. During our conversation, the subject came up of the recent moral failure of another great young leader in the same city, whose former members represented most of the growth in his new church.

At one point my friend posed the question, "Why do so many men quit and give up on all they believed in for so many years? After an awkward silence, the young leader, quoting from his mentor and movement leader said, "I was taught that the only thing needed to make it to the finish line is to sleep with my wife, spend my money, and build buildings." While on the surface it sounded like a good philosophy I must admit that I was taken aback at its shallowness. Such philosophy is precisely the mindset that leads to so many failures.

Simple phrases don't work in real life because life is anything but simple. While they may sound good and wise to some adoring young leaders in a moment, they are not any help when circumstances unfold that take the called of God into uncharted territories. It is a disservice to those seeking wisdom from leadership when we give answers that are not tested out and do not even reflect well in biblical experience. For instance, what does the leader do when neither he nor his wife want to sleep together? Or, what happens when other well meaning leaders and elders determine that you are not worth what you need to support your family? Finally, what happens when God Himself tells you not to build anything for Him anymore?

Most of those happened to King David. There came a point in David's life when his many spouses and concubines were not enough. You know the story; it led to his fall from grace and into one of the most difficult moments of his life. Obviously, he couldn't fight the temptation to stay faithful. And what about money? David was by all measures a man of great substance but everything he had was taken from him during his lifetime. Several times those who took from him were people close to him like king Saul or his son Absalom. He lived in caves, surviving like a nomad more than most realize. Finally, in David's desire to please God he decided to build God a tabernacle. After presenting God with his great plan God promptly declined and refused to allow David to build Him anything for the rest of his life.

To tell someone to simply build their whole life can lead to a huge number of buildings that are a testimony to man's foolish ego rather than to God. To be a good mentor, one must tell those he is leading the brutal truth. But the mentor must have first lived it. That is why young leaders are taught so much drivel. Their mentor either hasn't yet made the transition from visionary to dreamer or they are clueless as to how he made it. I contend that this lack of understanding of God's process has led to many throwing in the towel when that time arrives.

The time of the year had come for me to have my yearly physical. I was 50 years old at the time and because of my age I was required to go through many more tests than in previous years. Like most men, I loathe even the thought of this invasive process. On the appointed day, I sat before my doctor of 25 years filled with obvious anxiety and, after observing me for some time, he told me something that really shook me. He said, "Greg, while you were younger you could compensate for your physical weaknesses by sheer will and determination. Today marks the end of that lifestyle. Now you must deal with the root causes for these issues and make life changes that will fix the problem. Until then, we will have to prescribe some medicine that will help."

I left that office with pills in my hand and my mind racing with the implications of what he said. I had spent my whole life making things happen that I deemed important or God inspired. I held a philosophy that there was nothing I couldn't do or at least force to happen as long as I had breath in my lungs and a mouth to promote it. I say this to my discredit because history betrays the truth. Some of the goals I attempted to achieve and the plans I had were not even remotely of God. I just convinced myself and others they were. Again, His voice came to me as it had innumerable times, spoken without warning, with simple and life altering meaning. As usual, it came out of nowhere.

I was speaking to a dear friend, one of the toughest men I had ever known, a Navy SEAL, an intellectual, and a brilliant debater. We were talking, or should I say debating, about where the church is going and as always, we challenged one another to think out of the box regarding the future. That's when it came, that holy impartation with unmistakable tones that accentuate His voice.

In an instant, the Lord said these ominous words to me: "You are about to enter into the most difficult times of your life!"

Stupidly, I turned to my friend and told him what I heard, to which he said something that is typical of a warrior: "I'm glad it's you!" That day something began in my life that I can only describe as horrendously wonderful. Now, I am not some weirdo with a masochistic martyr complex but there is no other way I can explain it; however, let me make this part perfectly clear: the horrendous came long before the wonderful. I won't bore you with lengthy details but in short let me note some of my experiences over a two-year period. I lost my church, was diagnosed with skin cancer, lost all my income, lost my home, was diagnosed with severe nerve disorder, and broke both arms in a mountain bike accident. By far, the worst part of this time was the complete loss of identity with anything. For the first time in my life I was a man without a vision, seemingly a man at sea without oars or rudder, floating wherever the tides, winds, and waves took me. In short only God knew where I was going.

It all started with a look back over my life, wondering if what I had sowed my life into made any real difference. I cannot describe to you the depth of the feelings of failure that took me to the edge of life several times. I was angry at God for allowing me to waste so much of the one life I have to live and I paid Him back by not attending church, not praying, and not reading the Bible as I had every previous day of my life. Then, over time I began to miss Jesus! He had stripped away all the fluff in my relationship with Him.

I didn't need Him for a sermon or teaching for my church or a conference or for any professional purpose and all that was left was my first love. I just missed Him! I need to note that during all this time God never stopped loving me and providing for me. We were provided for supernaturally for more than three years without control of any organization. The conclusion was beginning to break through to me. God wanted something from me, or dare I say it, demanded something from me: SURRENDER! He desired absolute surrender of control of my life and its direction.

It was then that I came to know what it was like to live a life of grace, true grace, where I was the most undeserving person of His love, provision, and direction. It was then that in my death I was beginning to understand what it is like to know rebirth; not of my spirit but of the life that He wanted me to live. With that rebirth came something unexpected, a hatred for all the smoke and mirrors in the body of Christ. I hated the hype and the ungodly control I saw exhibited over the precious people of God. I hated the show of Sunday morning, where there was more of men then of God. I hated the fact that people would often come to meet Jesus and would leave having met a program void of His power.

Some of the bestselling books or e-books on leadership deal with some semblance of vision, and how to make the visionary successful. Those who buy the books are typically motivated and intelligent rip-snorting fellows who are looking for a program that will help them take on the world and win. For most of my ministry career I was that person! I consumed anything I could find on subjects that would allow me to achieve "the vision." If there was something that was working for someone else, I studied it and usually implemented it somewhere in my life and ministry.

The truth is that visionaries are an essential part of God's plan on the earth. I didn't think anything would get done in the world without the wisdom of these men because they are the drivers, negotiators, strategists, and the mystics of methodology. Looking back, I should have spent more time seeking God and less time seeking the ideas of men. But it is easier to follow men then to seek God and wait for His direction. The counsel of men never once taught me of the battle that is ever present when following God's path.

This is part of what motivates me to write. I want to save great warriors from philosophies and falsehoods that will cause them to be casualties rather than successful soldiers. I want to help every man I meet to make it to a good death, having found and achieved God's plan. I want to encourage those who are facing the inevitable time all visionaries face when God orders visions to die and dreams to begin. I have always believed that the best way to build is to do so from the end to the beginning and not the other way around. If the visionary would build with the end in sight for the entirety of his life, I think success is more than possible; knowing that the clock is ticking when visions will cease he will be much more careful in the process.

Many things lead one to embrace vision. The best possible vision comes by way of the heart of God transmuted to man through the Holy Spirit. Visions from God cause man to embrace the spirit of faith, which causes one to cast away all restraint to facilitate God's plan.

Scripture is full of stories of such men and women and specifically the book of Hebrews speaks of them. It is interesting that a vision that is truly from God works itself out in the great and the weak there is really no qualifying factor that can be identified in those God has used except that they were willing to lay down all, risk all, and face any obstacle to please God.

Vision can also be delegated. Delegated vision is what Noah gave to his family, Elijah gave to Elisha, and Paul gave to Timothy. I have found that those who carry delegated vision can range from those who have the same heart as the one who originally heard, to those who are only committed to the vision because of relational leverage.

Then there is vision that comes solely from man's ego. I find this kind of vision prevalent in the world as well as in the church today. It has the personality of ego written all over it. This kind of vision is the same type of vision that anyone, saved or not saved, would use to start a venture. One common factor revealing a vision that is ego-based, is the sign of one person's personality riddled throughout everything that is built. It is seen when everything that is done points back to the man who has the vision. It is seen when the most important agenda is self-focused as opposed to Christ-focused.

Several years ago I was attending a large meeting with hundreds of my friends and brothers. These were men I had stood with for at least a decade, men I respected and cared about deeply. One morning before the meeting I arrived a little late and sat in the back so I would not disturb anyone. I vividly remember the worship being very intense. It was during that time that the Lord spoke to me a phrase that shook me deeply. Like most words from God it came out of nowhere and at the time it didn't seem to make much sense to me. He said: "Behold the arrogance of vision!"

If I were to describe the main theme of the conference it would be how we were going to take the world for Jesus. We had it all down, even the year we would reach our goal of souls and more. In an innocent way, we were telling God all we would do for Him. Later we would realize that most likely He was looking at us with sadness and holy disdain because pride had found its way into our vision. It was not six months after that event that it all fell apart and with it the relationships of hundreds were thrown to the wind.

Vision is about one thing: the mind of God! It is not about charisma, hype, hyperbole, ranting, good shows, or great speaking. It is about the mind of God being placed into the flawed mind of a man to accomplish God's purposes on this earth. It is a holy impartation that the recipient is only a steward of as long as God's grace is upon him to carry it. Let all men know that the days of vision are numbered!

Rick Warren said, "Unfortunately, many leaders today start off as servants but end up as celebrities. They become addicted to attention, unaware that always being in the spotlight blinds you." This problem is not all the fault of the leader. It is also the fault of those who allow a good man to become enamored with himself by the worship of men. There is a major difference between following men who are duly appointed by God and the worship of these men. There is no doubt in my mind that the church has been guilty of the worship of men and their agendas a great deal more than the worship of God and His!

Throughout the ages we have propped up men to the place of "leadership" because we have been told in Scripture that we are supposed to have men of God lead us. All too often we have made men the recipient of the glory only Christ deserves and men in their pride have accepted it more then they have rejected it. This is the reason we are living in times where the power of God is rarely seen. God simply cannot trust men with His power because we always attempt to control it, make a movement out of it, or worse, contain it.

The disciples, the first recipients of God's true power in the New Testament, never attempted to control or contain it. Their Spirit-led response was to get out of the way and make themselves servants to what He was doing. They humbly carried the most precious substance on earth, God's anointing, with an open hand. They died without a building or statue depicting their image. They died a good death.

As a result, their lives continue as examples of how to steward what is most precious to God. They showed us that the power of God is given to those who refuse to hold it close, or to pollute it with self. Today the world is looking for men worthy of following. Men who are filled with the power of God and that in humility will resist all forms of ownership of what God allows them to steward in His grace.

What are the attributes of a man worthy of following? A man who knows, declares, and lives like he is just a man. A man who knows what it is like to wash the feet of those he has the privilege to lead. A man who walks humbly before God and fights with all his might the control of the people while letting them know that he is not there to lead them to his vision but rather to God's. He is a man who knows how to get out of the way, out of the limelight, out of the glory, and hand it to others while making sure the people are not following him. He is a man willing to lay down his life and all that encompasses to serve the people.

It is easy to identify what has been built on pride. A postmortem of fallen leaders and movements can show that the signs were everywhere and plain to see if those around were only willing to see it. Just look at the end, and pride is revealed: the end of pride is always a fall! The worst thing about this fall is what happens to those who gave their most precious treasure to facilitate what was built on the fault line of ego and pride. They are left empty, untrusting, and disillusioned. They are taken out of the battle.

Men without pride serve without selfishness or pretense. They don't demand things from the people they are called to serve. They offer what they have determined to be the will of God to the people and then leave it up to God to confirm that path. Men without pride are listeners and responders. My favorite example of this is in the wonderful story of Noah. He wasn't in the game for people. He was all about God and what He wanted whether it made sense or not. Men without pride are not afraid to reveal their own faults. I love it when Paul told the people: "I am the least among you." And he meant it! Paul spent time meditating on his unworthiness to hold what was precious to God.

Most today would think this to be a practice of weakness but I think it is just the opposite. When a man spends his personal time in prayer naked and exposed before God the result is God's trust. John the Baptist did something that should serve to be an example of what leads to becoming a great leader. When John saw Jesus and recognized Him to be the One he was prophesying about, his immediate response to his followers was to tell them to leave him and follow Jesus.

When was the last time you heard a man say that to his congregation? When was the last time you heard an inept and disgraced politician or corporate executive say to his constituents or employees to go and follow another? It almost never happens because men are drunk on their own power or glory. While the worship of men is dangerous, even more dangerous is being anywhere near the man who allows others to worship him.

Get over yourself! Realize that you are a steward of everything and the owner of nothing. We will all answer to God for how we conducted ourselves during our lifetime. If you live like a steward, you will make decisions that reveal the thoughtfulness of one who knows that a day of accounting will come. To die a good death is to choose a life that centers upon others and not you.

CHAPTER 7

A GOOD DEATH

"Be ashamed to die until you have won some victory for humanity."

Horace Mann

My entrance into the ministry was marked with the confidence that I could really make a difference. I envisioned being part of a community of believers who reflected the ideals and courage of the "cloud of witnesses" we read about in the book of Hebrews. However, after more than two decades in ministry, including speaking in many nations, traveling around the world, and striving to help people, a vague, unsettled feeling stalked me. I felt as if little I had accomplished made much of a difference.

When I shared my feelings with several friends, they shrugged it off with comments that I was in a midlife crisis, telling me that I shouldn't be so self-critical and things would get better. The easy thing would be to agree but something inside me rejected the counsel. You see, I believed God had placed this discontent within me. If we are going to be good warriors, then we need to trust our inner voice. It is not always depression when we are feeling down. Sometimes something is wrong and needs to change.

As I continued asking Him for wisdom, it became clear that He wanted me to understand that my discontent from a heavenly perspective meant that He wanted to change my view both of the past and my future. And the message He wanted me to know was that what I had accomplished to this point was nothing compared to what He had planned for me. That wake-up call made it clear to me that it was time to shake my world!

One particular day I awoke intending to hit the gym for a morning workout. It was a typical, sun-kissed Southern California day. Light breezes blew in from the Pacific Ocean as early morning rays bounced off our bedroom window. Salt-tinged air invigorated my lungs.

An early riser, I had already planned my schedule from morning to bedtime. That is, until I received a call from a close friend and active Navy SEAL. He said, "Greg, we've got an emergency with one of the guys at the drop zone and I need you to come down here right away!"

The drop zone is where skydivers meet for jump exercises. Psyched up that day for an invigorating workout, followed by a long list of tasks on my "to do" list, I sighed, shook my head, dressed, and headed for the field. When I arrived, I sensed something was amiss. Numerous SEALs lingered in their jump attire, smiling, chatting and obviously not upset about an emergency. Suddenly a wave of indignation came over me. I had been set up!

The week before, in a Bible study with a number of these special forces warriors who either belong to our church or visit regularly, I confessed to a fear of heights. "There are some fears we just have to live with," I said. In retrospect, I can't believe I exposed myself to them like that. Not to a group of men who live on the edge, never accepting fear as a deterrent to completing their mission! After spending most of my years avoiding high places, I had no intentions of overcoming that fear. I felt quite at peace about taking this path of least resistance. However, this day the guys quickly made their intentions clear. Handing me a jump suit, a small cordon of skydivers ushered me toward an airplane.

My mind raced with all the reasons why this was a really bad idea and I thought of numerous excuses and logical reasons to stop their plans.   My wife depends on me. What is she going to think about me risking my life like this? I'm the father of five children, most of whom are still at home. They need me around. I'm a pastor. I have a responsibility to my congregation to live and not die.

I am not sure if the fright in my eyes exposed the frenzied excuses cascading around my brain, but it wasn't going to deter my hardy band of encouragers. In what seemed like a really bad nightmare, soon about 12 of us were boarding the plane dressed in jump suits, helmets, and goggles. The plane took off and hurtled into the sky. Our aging plane had no doors to protect us from the rapidly increasing expanse of air between us and the ground. Once we reached 12,000 feet—someone blared the heart-pounding news of our ascent over the loudspeaker—a guy behind me barked, "Okay! Scoot to the door! On the count of three we jump!"

Terror gripping my insides, my knees shook as I wobbled toward the door. I wondered when the film of my life would flash before my eyes. But "three" never came. On the count of "two" I found myself in a heart-pumping free fall. I still have no clue what initially went through my mind as I sailed through the air. It was not a static line jump, meaning that we were in a free fall for some time before the parachute opened. Then, seemingly out of nowhere, my friend Jeff, flew up beside me and grabbed my hand. He smiled and soon screamed at me something like, "Way to go dude!" After we landed, I fought dizziness and nausea for several minutes. However, once those feelings passed, I surprised myself when I said, "Hey, let's do that again!"

The Dawning of a New Personal Era

That day God began the shaking of my "life." I cannot tell you how great it felt to overcome that fear. It wasn't just the jump that gave me a sense of victory. During my chaotic fall God let me know that He will not tolerate me accepting anything that will hinder His course for my life. He told me my destiny is much different than I imagined and that it was about to enter into a difficult time of transition. He expected me to rise to the challenges He would unfold. Either I choose to face my fears, excuses, and mediocrity, or God will force me to face them. While I overcame my fear of heights, many more await me.

When we commit to God to be His warriors, He commits to keep us in the fight, which includes moving us when we are not aware of what is going on. My testimony reveals that God loves us more then we will ever know. And when He sees things in our lives that will cause us to lose the fighting spirit He will stir things up in a big way. Living by faith is a wonderful life. At this point in our lives, my wife and I have the perspective of experience to draw from. Almost 40 years ago we made the decision to live by faith in EVERY area of our lives as best we could.

Looking back, I can tell you that it is a wild ride but one that I would not want any other way. The good news is that at 60 years old I am still in the fight. Through grace I have been preserved. It is something that could never be accomplished without divine intervention. Warriors often move! They are not the ones who determine times and places. They receive orders and do whatever is needed to complete them. Our most recent move came when we received orders to move yet again.

The difficult part about moving is convincing my wife it is right. In our marriage of almost four decades we have moved more than 25 times, but this move was different. We weren't just moving to a different part of the city. This time, to make this move, we would have to sell everything, load up the truck and camper, leave our children and grandchildren, and move from beautiful San Diego to middle Tennessee.

The mission: to open a center for the support of soldiers at Fort Campbell, which is both in Tennessee and Kentucky. I am blessed to be married to a woman who is a warrior. She is both beauty and beast. When she agrees with something, she leaves no doubt. But if she is in disagreement, nothing can change her mind. I hate to admit it but long ago I became more afraid of her than any of my mentors and counselors. It was not unlike me to come home at the end of the day with crazy ideas about plans for us, expecting her to just submit to my idea and move. After that worked twice, it never happened again. She learned very quickly how to be the wife of a visionary.

My wife is a horse enthusiast. And she often leaves the house with the clang of her horse spurs. She is used to riding a horse that weighs more than one thousand pounds and making it do whatever she wants despite her petite 120-pound frame. She is fearless and God gave her as a gift to me, although I will admit that this "gift" didn't always feel like one. Especially when it came to me telling her what God had said to me. Every time I would come home and say, "God told me," she would come back with, "Great! When He tells me the same thing I will get back to you." I hated that phrase, but it was the right one. She has saved us more misery over the years by sticking to the value of agreement. If we are going to agree then we both have to hear the Spirit.

When God spoke to me about moving to Tennessee, I expected a fight. I was sure she was going to fight me about it. All five of our children lived in San Diego, along with our grandchildren. Also, all our friends were there and her horses. So when I told her about what I felt God was leading us to I was shocked when it only took about five minutes for her to reply, "So when are we leaving?"

I vividly remember shutting the door of our truck, which was loaded to the hilt, and looking back in the mirror to see our adult daughter and one of our sons holding each other while watching us go. I looked at my wife and smiled, and we never looked back again. To us, we were responding to orders and it was up to God to take care of everything ahead and what we were leaving behind.

Fort Campbell is home to thousands of soldiers. It supports the third largest military population in the Army and the seventh largest in the Department of Defense. Fort Campbell is home to the Screaming Eagles of the 101st Airborne Division (Air Assault). It is also home to 5th Special Forces Group (ABN), 160th Special Operations Aviation Regiment (SOAR), 31st Military Police Detachment, 58th Aviation Regiment, 1st Battalion, 61st Engineer Battalion, 95th Maintenance Company, 101st Support Group (Corps), 249th Engineer Battalion, and 902nd Military Intelligence Group. The Air Force has two units at Campbell Army Airfield: 19th Air Support Operation Squadron and 621st Air Mobility Operations Group.

Fort Campbell is also home to a 92% divorce rate and an alarmingly high suicide rate. It is a virtual war zone for the families of those who serve our nation. When God called us to leave San Diego and move to Tennessee, He was calling us to go to battle facing the enemy destroying the families of our soldiers. As we drove into town I had no idea how we were going to accomplish our mission, but we knew that as long as we had faith in our hearts and followed His lead it was just a matter of time.

Fast forward to now: we have a 12-acre center that serves as a staging point for the training of men and women who are trained to fight the demon that is destroying the families of our soldiers. It also is a healing center for families who are wounded. There is much more I want to say about the Force Center but instead I want to share something personal. When we drove away from San Diego most of our children were struggling. It seemed somewhat uncaring for us to leave them in that condition and move two thousand miles away from them to help other families when our own family was in trouble.

But it was not our call! We were given orders and we were going to follow them. Everything else was God's problem. One of the amazing things about living by faith is you get to be a spectator in the arena of God's grace. You get to see that with every move of obedience you take God matches it and exceeds expectation with a move that blows your mind.

Today every one of our children and grandchildren are doing amazing. Just two years after our departure from San Diego, each of their lives has been transformed by God. A warrior's life is one of faith, and while a move of faith never promises ease involves moving into the unknown, it is the best life one can live on earth.

Scripture tells us that we go from "glory to glory," which to many of us translates into a promise that we will go from one level of good life to another level of good life. It is interesting that few of us want to acknowledge there is a price to every new level of glory that cannot be attained unless the process of chance, sacrifice, and struggle is navigated correctly.

I am certain that those who quit on God all have one thing in common. They entered the struggle for the next level of glory and refused to accept the cost to attain it. The fact is there is a huge cost to forward movement in our faith. We have to face uncertainty, we have to accept the fact that what was once acceptable in our lives no longer will make the standard. We have to face fears, accept responsibility for our actions, and buck up to the challenge of a new day. God initiates these challenges through unique means. My experience tells me that God brings His people to crisis before each new level of glory.

CHAPTER 8

THE SPIRIT OF THE LION "UNTIL LAMBS BECOME LIONS"

Coronado Island was my hangout. We held Bible studies in the BUD/s barracks and ministered to many of the sailors who called that island home. I was there almost daily and loved the time I was allowed to speak to those great men and their families. One beautiful morning I was having coffee at a cafe on Orange Street when I received a call from the officer of a SEAL unit asking if I had time to meet with him that day. I sensed an urgency in his voice so I asked him to meet me soon at the café. He was the commanding officer of a team where three-quarters of its members had come to Christ under our ministry. He was also an avowed atheist.

Since he couldn't deny the benefit he was seeing in his men's lives and their families, he decided to ask me to tell him what I had been communicating to his men. He started by thanking me for helping his men and their families, transitioning very quickly into what felt like an interrogation. A Naval academy graduate and a brilliant communicator, he didn't hold back what he believed or didn't believe. He spoke for more than forty-five minutes about his reasons for not believing in a god. One of his main issues with God, and specifically Christianity, was the idea that the God of our faith was not even able to save Himself from the cross. It was completely unacceptable to him that Christ was able to do all He did on earth, healing the sick, raising the dead, and more, and then not be able to save Himself.

I listened intently and commented little until he seemed to be ready for my response. One thing that has been so wonderful about ministering to military men is that they almost always speak frankly, pulling no punches when telling you what they think. But I have noticed if you can answer their questions with a lucid and clear answer, even if it conflicts with theirs, they will give it due consideration and possibly change their position. In my response to the commander I began by telling him that he really had a misconception of who Christ was and why He came to this earth. Then I began to speak in a language he would relate to. I said that Christ came to the earth to fulfill a mission. His orders were to be a lamb and to take upon Himself the sins of all men. I made it clear that at any time Christ could have turned his tormentors into chickens if He wanted but that would be in direct opposition to His mission.

Then I spoke about the pain He endured, willingly accepting that pain as an act of love for the very people who tormented Him. I said that in today's military, His actions would have without question earned Him the Medal of Honor. Then suddenly, I noticed the commander's face begin to change. He was not asking questions but was seemingly in deep thought. I remained quiet. Before long he looked me eye to eye and said that while he still had many questions he was convinced that Jesus was the only savior and accepted Christ into his life.

To this day he and his wife continue to serve Christ and our country. A year later while having lunch with him, he said something very encouraging to me. He recounted that moment at the café in Coronado and our discussions. Then he said that it wasn't just what I said to him that convinced him to become a believer. He said that the deepest impact on him was seeing what happened to his SEAL teammates after they received Christ. He said that the changes in those men for the better could not be possible unless there was a real God. All glory belongs to Him.

You may say, "Jesus is the Lamb of God! Isn't this Lamb the head of the church?" True, but look at reality. The lamb isn't the most valiant of creatures. Lambs are passive, lack any fighting instinct, and are easy prey. But the mission required God to come with the spirit of a lamb. As the Lamb of God, Christ came into the world to redeem humankind. He submitted to torture and suffering because it was necessary to be the conclusive sacrifice. The key word though is, *was*. The Lamb finished His work and now sits in heaven, victorious over evil. A friend of mine, Dr. Les Breitman MD, notes: "It is of interest to contrast the lion and the lamb characteristics of Christ. As Lion He is sovereign; He is judge; He is majesty. The lion speaks of the government of God, just as the tribe of Judah governed Israel. The lamb speaks of meekness and of salvation by His sacrifice, as the lamb had long ago been ordained for sacrifice in the traditions of the Jews. So the lamb characteristic refers to His first coming, whereas the lion speaks of the Second Advent." In other words, Christ awaits His next return to the earth to reveal Himself as the victorious Christ bearing the heart of the lion!"

Given this truth, it is essential that the church take on the spirit, not of His first coming, but of His second coming. In Revelation 6:2, John wrote, "And I looked, and behold, a white horse, and he who sat on it had a bow; and a crown was given to him; and he went out conquering, and to conquer." I don't believe Christ intended for His church to identify with the lamb or emulate its meek spirit after His ascension to heaven. C.H. Spurgeon said: "Beloved, in fighting with sin without and within, with error doctrinal or practical, with spiritual wickedness in high places or low places, with devils and the devil's allies, you are waging Jehovah's war, and unless He himself can be worsted, you need not fear defeat. Quail not before superior numbers, shrink not from difficulties or impossibilities, flinch not at wounds or death, smite with the two-edged sword of the Spirit, and the slain shall lie in heaps. The battle is the Lord's and He will deliver His enemies into our hands."

Matthew Henry states: "Is not our religion much more a warfare? It is so; for we struggle with the opposition of the powers of darkness, and with many enemies who would keep us from God and heaven. We have enemies to fight against, a captain to fight for, a banner to fight under, and certain rules of war by which we are to govern ourselves. Now it is requisite that a soldier be both stout-hearted and well armed."

Understanding what Christ actually did on the cross is essential to the needed transformation in the church today. Throughout the years, the idea of what actually happened during the crucifixion has been relegated to a custom and has, at best, been watered down. When Christ was born in the manger to Mary and Joseph, He was born with a mandate, or order, within. Simply put, He was born to die! He was born to die a good death. Yes, He lived a life before us that was miraculous and awe inspiring, but virtually everything He did was in the spirit of the Lamb. Because only a lamb could truly represent the sacrificial standard required to take on the sins of humanity and provide a path to eternal life.

The Lamb finished His mission. He found a good death. But because He found a good death, He also found a good resurrection. When Christ rose from the dead, He was no longer acting as a Lamb. He was the victorious Christ, worthy of all praise. No longer a Lamb, He would now begin another battle. One that is exercised every second of every day on behalf of His church. He sits at the right hand of the Father, ever making intercession for His beloved people. That warfare for man will go on until He returns as the Lion. This moment will mark the end of the fight to all those who call Him Lord. But until then, we fight!

Maintaining a Battle Posture

Posture is everything to us if we are going to overcome in this life. Because the devil roams around like a roaring lion seeking whom he may devour, our situational awareness both in the spiritual and natural cannot be overstated. What is your present posture in life? The noun "posture" refers to a particular approach or attitude. Attitude is everything if we want to demonstrate a life of success. To live passively by just letting life happen and taking no particular position on things, is to accept a life that guarantees you will change nothing. This includes you. But if we approach life with an attitude of conviction and resolve, we will change things for the better.

In Daniel 10, we read that he took a stand as a result of a vision he had received. His posture was one of a warrior as he stood the test of patience and self-doubt and remained unmovable. What is interesting, is that God sent the answer to his prayer the first day he uttered it. However, the angel who was sent to bring the answer was detained in battle in the spirit realm. Instead of placing a time limit on the answer, he believed in his convictions enough to refuse to give in.

The man who has taken a posture of conviction until his prayer is answered is unmatched by any adversary. Conversely, the man who takes no stand is at the mercy of all adversaries. I'm sure it is no surprise to you that today's society is rife with men of no conviction or posture. From politicians to parents, and preachers, more often than not, they tell us one thing and live out another. I can assure you that this is not living. Posture is the gift a man gives to himself and to those he loves.

God never gives you a dream, and enlists you in a fight, that He is not committed to fulfilling. You have a part in that process.

We have to come to terms with the fact that there is more happening in our lives in the spirit than what is visible. If fact, there is still more to be discovered about God than He has revealed so far, and that includes in Scripture.

For instance, when Jesus took the disciples to the Mount of Transfiguration, the supernatural met them there. Suddenly Jesus was transfigured before them, and two other beings, Moses and Elijah, stood talking with Him. Then a Voice spoke from above and communicated to Peter, James, and John. What was communicated elicits more questions, not only to the disciples hearing the words, but also to all who would read them to this day.

Think about it: Jesus was transfigured. This literally means that He changed into matter that was not human. Someone PLEASE explain that one to me scientifically. And what about Moses and Elijah? They were otherworldly, and were also not of matter known to this world, even to this day.

I want to ask you to get used to pushing your limits of understanding by learning to question things. Especially question those traditional ideas you have always believed of the Bible. If you want to be blown away read the Bible to ask questions. I guarantee it will change you into a better person. By the way, don't take the easy way out and let others give their answers to you. As John 10:27 says "My sheep listen to my voice; I know them, and they follow me." This literally means that if you are one of Jesus' sheep then you are actually able to hear His voice. It doesn't matter if you haven't recognized it yet, the fact is He is speaking and you are receiving. You just need to continue to ask your questions until the communication is clear.

God spoke from heaven to three men who each heard the same thing. "This is my beloved Son, hear Him." What does "hear Him" mean? What instigated this meeting? While most are happy answering these questions with ethereal answers like, "That is just God," or "We cannot know the ways of God," I wonder if we shouldn't be attempting to discover the answers because God wants us to. Is it possible that there is a scientific breakthrough hidden in this encounter?

What about the discovery of another dimension inhabited by beings not made of matter from this world? The fact that there are angels, demons, and other spirit beings means that in order for us to realize reality the way God intended, we must push the envelope to discovery. If we are to fight the good fight of faith, which Paul the apostle tells us cannot be known by any of our five senses, we cannot truly fight unless we seek truth outside the obvious.

Are You a Warrior?

Does a warrior cry? Does a warrior bleed? Does a warrior fall? Does a warrior quit?

Are you a warrior? Jesus didn't cry. He wept. Jesus didn't bleed. His blood was spilt. Jesus didn't fall. His body was broken. All men cry. Most hide it. Warriors don't hide it. They have nothing to be ashamed of because they leave it all on the battlefield. All men bleed. Most hide it. Warriors don't hide it. They were wounded in battle and everyone comes out of battle changed. All men fall. Most hide it. Warriors don't hide it. They are strong and stand up again for the next fight.

All men quit. Almost everyone hides it because they are weak. Warriors don't quit. Warriors are not mere men. They have a vision for the future and understand the situations of the present with great knowledge of the past. We are in war and warriors don't quit. Yes, warriors cry! Yes, warriors bleed! Yes, warriors fall! No, warriors do not quit!

Are you a warrior?

Of all the questions that can be asked about a warrior, there is only one that comes back with a negative answer. A warrior never quits. Never! Mediocrity has been championed since the dawn of time. King David's brothers believed he should have stayed in the fields and tended the sheep. Instead he led Israel to victory. The apostle Peter was beaten and told to never speak about Jesus again. Yet he died for and became a pillar of the church.

Where are the warriors? Are they even around? Do you see them? Are you a warrior? As Ephesians 6:10-12 states, "Finally, be strong in the Lord and in his mighty power. Put on the full armor of God so that you can take your stand against the devil's schemes. For our struggle is not against flesh and blood, but against the rulers, against the authorities, against the powers of this dark world and against the spiritual forces of evil in the heavenly realms."

What makes a warrior? Commitment makes a warrior. This causes the soul to desire strong fellowship with the Lord, which defies the path of least resistance that the body enjoys. Most are not warriors because they are weak. They are not wearing the armor to protect the body, so the body gets beat up causing the undisciplined mind to quit.

As Ephesians 6:13-20 states, "Therefore put on the **full armor of God** so that when the day of evil comes, you may be able to stand your ground, and *after you have done everything, to stand. Stand firm* then, with the **belt of truth** buckled around your waist, with the **breastplate of righteousness** in place, and with your **feet fitted with the readiness** that comes from the gospel of peace. In addition to all this, take up the **shield of faith**, with which you can extinguish all the flaming arrows of the evil one. Take the **helmet of salvation** and the **sword of the Spirit**, which is the word of God. And **pray in the Spirit on all occasions** with all kinds of prayers and requests. With this in mind, be alert and always keep on praying for the saints."

A Phone Call with a Demon

Like most women, my wife is really good at listing things that need to be done around the house. Her idea of a "task" is to build a barn or paint the entire upstairs. I almost always respond to her request like this: "Honey, I will look at my schedule and get back to you."

That usually works for about a week and then she begins the verbal reminders. Essentially, she has learned the way to motivate me to do tasks that I deem low priority is to make me so fed up with hearing about it, that I do it.

Side note: It is impossible for me to open a can of paint without it getting all over the place. Once I take on a painting job it is guaranteed that not only will the walls get painted but just about everything else near the work area will too. When the job is done, I have to spend more time cleaning up my mess then I did on the job.

With that in mind, this particular day I was panting the upstairs and about half way done when I received a phone call from a number I didn't know. For some stupid reason I answered it, painting my iPhone in the process. I quickly attached my headset and began talking. The person on the other end was someone I had once known and I quickly began to tell him that I was unable to speak due to my circumstance.

Now, I want to warn you that I am about to take you into a conversation with a demon. And with that I am going to tell you what the demon said and how I responded. My reason is not to give airtime to the lies of a devil but to show you by example what posture means. The voice on the other end responded to my request to speak later by saying, "No pastor, you will talk to me now."

Having not yet realized that the man was demon-possessed and not wanting to offend, I said okay, I would try. He then began to tell me that what he was about to say was intended to teach me something I really needed regarding my understanding of God. He said that, followed by the statement, "I have more wisdom than you could obtain in many lifetimes." He then told me that he was more than a thousand years old. Because I was postured correctly I discerned correctly. I knew that I wasn't just dealing with drugs, alcohol, or a psychological disorder. In thirty years of counseling I can tell when someone is suffering from such issues. This was undoubtedly a demon.

Now most people at this point would just hang up the phone. But a man who is postured for battle doesn't run when the enemy shows up. If anyone was going to hang up it was the devil. He then asking me a question. "Is the devil a man or a woman?" Side note: Remember that being postured correctly requires that we not only be able to stand against darkness but we need to know the strategy for dealing with the wiles of the devil.

Since I was speaking to a demon it was necessary that I fight him on spiritual terms. My response to his question was a blunt, "I don't care!" Since that answer didn't give him anywhere to go he made a statement. "The Bible is a children's book. In my one thousand years I know that real truth cannot be found in that book." I said, "Sorry, you are wrong." It was then that he began to emphatically demand that I listen to what he was telling me because he was not wrong. When I told the demon that his opinion on life was not going to change one thing in me, he began to get verbally abusive. It was then that I told him to take all his opinions along with his attitude and go to hell. The next thing I heard was a click. Sweet! Posture is the only reason I was prepared to fight this fight. It felt good to give one of Satan's imps a beating!

CHAPTER 9

LOVE AND HATE

Nowhere is the love of God for people and the wrath of God against sin more clearly revealed than at the cross. It was there that the Father sacrificed His Son. From that moment man would have a choice regarding the life he would live and where he would spend eternity. Because of Christ's sacrifice on the cross we are spared the hate and judgment of the Father. The death man would ultimately face would be of his own choosing for the first time. We know that God is love. But love without hate is not true love. One cannot completely love righteousness and truth and not hate their opposites. Many think it is impossible for one to conceive of hate being demonstrated by a God of love. However, God reveals hatred throughout the Bible.

Perhaps the closest we can come to imagining God's love is to consider our affection for our own little children. We adore them and will do anything to make them happy and safe. Yet the very thought of someone intentionally trying to harm or steal one of them away quickly reveals the flip side of that crazy love to be passionate, intense anger that without a moment's hesitation would cause you to put your life between them and harm's way.

Love and grace, justice and anger—they're like two sides of the same coin. If you camp out on one attribute of the divine nature (love or anger) to the exclusion of the other, the result is a very distorted understanding of God. That, in turn, creates a distorted understanding of Christian discipleship—what it means to be Christ-like. Christians commonly talk about being motivated by the love of God to serve, give, or sacrifice.

As we should, we will pray regularly asking for His love to fill us, to consume us, and to shine through us. But to what extent are you motivated, impassioned, and consumed by your sense of what God hates? The apostle Paul wrote to the Roman church: "Let love be without hypocrisy. Abhor what is evil; cling to what is good" (Romans 12:9). We seem to be a lot better at clinging to good than we are the abhorring part. Perhaps it is because as modern-day, Western Christians we have emphasized the love and mercy of God to the exclusion of those other aspects of the divine nature—namely God's anger and wrath aimed at injustice and particularly aimed at those who mistreat the helpless and innocent. The result of this distorted perception of God is that Christians turn out to be timid, passionless, and indifferent when it comes to taking a stand against evil and injustice in our society. God used one major encounter in my life to challenge my own passivity and indifference.

As the pastor of a church in San Diego, California, I frequently went out to meet with members. I always preferred to engage them on their turf, not at the church. On one particular day, the meeting with a church member was quite extraordinary because it took place at the training center for U.S. Navy SEALs. In the middle of my grand tour I was introduced to a Navy SEAL. He was an exceptional young man but an unbeliever who (I soon came to realize) deeply resented my presence on his base.

The only demonstration of Christianity he had seen was characterized by weakness, timidity, and retreat in the face of evil. Here was a man who had dedicated his life to duty, honor, and decisive action. He had a crystal-clear sense of right and wrong and a quick willingness to sacrifice his life when called upon. Noting that I was a pastor, he asked, "What are you doing here?" His glaring stare seemed to say, "How dare you bring that kind, weak-willed indifference into this place!"

His challenge provoked an angry response in me, but I was not at all angry with him. Jesus was the supreme model of all those characteristics he valued, and I was angry at how my Lord had been misrepresented. At the same time, I felt great compassion for that young warrior and others like him. Standing eye to eye with that soldier, I prayed, "God help me reach these men!" Within a short time, I had resigned from my church to begin working with these amazing people who protect the innocent and put it all on the line on a daily basis for others. They know what it is like to passionately love and at the same time passionately hate. Most of the time the only thing missing is the connection of those emotions to Jesus Christ.

The very idea that God can hate or even condone it in Christians stirs up deep emotion, as it should. A shallow glance of this possibility can leave one to dismiss the idea all together. But truth rarely dwells in the shallows. Almost all believers living today have seen religions declare God's hate to justify their actions. There is not a day that goes by that we do not hear the news of some horrible atrocity conducted by those who follow the false God of Islam. The justification for the abhorrent acts of radical Islam is that God hates. The irony of all this is the false claim that Islam is a religion of peace. But there is not a single shred of evidence to verify that claim.

In all fairness though, Christianity has a history of doing the same. During the Dark Ages, it was common for priests claiming to represent Jesus to stand at the gates and declare, "Death to the infidel." Men carried out atrocities because of these priests who had convinced the people that they were the voice of God. Slavery was condoned since it was declared as one's Christian duty to own slaves. White supremacy was born out of this same justification. Those who espoused such ideas were no more Christian than Islamist. But they all had one thing in common: They misrepresented God to the people and defiled His holy faith. In fact, more evil has been done in the name of God than in any other.

Due to the misuse of the word *hate* as it relates to God, many discount it entirely as a part of the Christian experience. But God's hatred is well documented in Scripture. Solomon wrote the following in Proverb 6:16-18, making it impossible to believe otherwise: "There are six things which the LORD hates, Yes, seven which are an abomination to Him: Haughty eyes, a lying tongue, and hands that shed innocent blood, a heart that devises wicked plans, feet that run rapidly to evil, a false witness who utters lies, and one who spreads strife among brothers." God will never change His mind regarding any of these issues, ever. Therefore, it must be concluded that hate has a place in the Christian experience even after the death and resurrection of Christ.

Witnessing Jesus making a whip, and then going to overturn the money-changers' tables, driving them out of the temple, His disciples may have been a little bewildered. I would think they could be feeling a bit like the proverbial martial arts student who once said to his master, "You teach me fighting but you talk about peace. How do you reconcile the two?" The master replied, "It is better to be a warrior in the garden than to be a gardener in a war."

John's Gospel says, "His disciples remembered that it was written, "Zeal for Your house will consume Me" (Psalms 69:9, John 2:17). So, what do you love, what do you hate, what are you so passionate about that you cannot help but take a stand? We are to hate what God hates and cling to what is good. It is impossible to really hate something and not be doing something about it. How many times do we utter the words, "I hate?" But do we?

If one really hates being overweight, then one is making the necessary changes needed to become fit. Otherwise you really don't hate being overweight. If you hate being sickly, then you will make the life changes necessary to become healthy. Otherwise you really don't hate being sickly. If you really hate something, that fact is revealed in your own actions against what you hate. But if we are going to engage hate correctly then we must be aware of the potential for its abuse.

As I alluded to earlier, the tenth and eleventh centuries marked a period called the Dark Ages. Its history shows us what a society can become when a people give their consciences over to a hierarchy or an institution instead of the Holy Spirit. Our conscience is one of our most precious treasures God has given us. It must be carefully protected and constantly watched over to keep pure. It is through those pure consciences that God can entrust both His love and hate.

Also, there are times when the church as a whole maintains a consensus regarding something God hates. An example is the murder of the unborn. God hates what is happening to millions of children and He expects the church to take action to stop it. But there are limits of what we can do with what God hates. And those limits are exceeded when we become what God hates in our attempts to deal with what God hates. In the Dark Ages the Roman Catholic Church became the very manifestation of what God hates while at the same time justifying its actions in the name of God.

One example of this is the Inquisition. This scheme was designed to inquire into the spread of heresy and to call before its tribunal Catholics suspected of heresy with a view to securing their repentance. The accused were sometimes tortured and even put to death. The Inquisition was a disgrace to men who call themselves followers of God. Another is in the practice of simony. Simony was the sinful practice of giving or obtaining an appointment to a church office for money. This was a common practice in the Middle Ages, even in the obtaining of the office of pope.

Learning from history, we must exercise the greatest caution, both when we determine what God hates and also, what measures should be taken to deal with it. The safe equation is this: We will always make a correct determination if we look at the world through God's love. It is through His love that we will become His snipers of what He hates. We should not be afraid to act when God's hatred is obvious, and there is no better place to begin than with ourselves.

Beginning My Fight

The main reason why men are not engaged in the battle is because so many suffer from debilitating guilt from their present and past sins. The very thought of being used by God is torture because we are so aware of our unworthiness. So, let's talk about it! There is sin and there is habitual sin. Sin is unavoidable in this world. No one is perfect and Christ never asserted otherwise. It is because of this that we are given the means to forgiveness when we fall. Then there is habitual sin. This is the dangerous side of sin because it means that we have come to the place where a particular sin has become part of us.

If we are not careful to deal with this kind of sin when it has taken hold then we are in danger of having our conscience seared, rendering us incapable of engagement in the battle. Now I realize that some reading this may acknowledge that this is already the case. One may have tapped out succumbing to hopelessness. But remember this absolute in the character of Christ: He never changes! This means that no sin, habitual or not, is beyond His forgiveness. That is not to say that there are not consequences to sin. Depending upon how long and how far you have taken habitual sin, there may be a lifelong effect.

When we are truly repentant of sin, there is nothing God will not forgive us of. Nothing! Many who are guilt-ridden and rife with self-condemnation are that way because they were not directed to a warfare in the beginning of their walk with Christ. As I mentioned earlier, when I was in my early teens my mother contracted a disease called scleroderma, which essentially made her skin turn hard, causing excruciating pain and ultimately death. She lived for two years after her diagnosis. When she was nearing death, we were called to her bedside one by one to say goodbye. I will never forget the last moments I had with her.

Just before she breathed her last breath, in a semi-delusional state, she cried out in prayer to God saying, "God, please don't let me die. I want to be with my family." Shortly thereafter, she passed away at 37. I cannot tell you how deep her final prayer affected me as a young man. But I know that its impact stayed with me for more than a decade. When I was saved, I remember struggling deeply with what I saw others so easily experience. I remember watching praise, worship, and prayer come so easily for most. For me, it seemed impossible.

I was easily distracted and felt something gnawing at me every time I was in that environment. I was jealous of these people and felt that either God was not wanting to be close to me or that I had a problem locking myself out of His presence. It is hard to admit today, but I continued to grow in my faith in spite of this condition. I became good at acting like I had it all together and over the years I just accepted it as my lot in life.

At some point I was included in church leadership, which included invitations to conferences on leadership development. I enjoyed these conferences once they got over the praise and worship. At one particular conference I attended, the main focus was on praise and worship. It was not only the main subject but the main activity of the three-day event. The first day was uneventful. But the second day I noticed a deep stirring, like something ominous was going to happen. I couldn't seem to block it out of my mind and toward the end of day, a break was called.

I left my notebook on my seat and began making my way toward the aisle when a woman whom I'd never met stopped me and asked if she could have a few minutes of my time. She then began to describe to me the circumstances surrounding my mother's death and my reaction in graphic detail, including the moments after my mother's funeral when everyone gathered at my home.

I remember resenting them for no particular reason. People kept hugging me and telling me it was going to be okay and that they would be there for me if I ever needed them. But inside I cringed. So, my way of dealing with it was to crawl into my closet and close the door. I stayed there for the next two hours.

During that time in my closet, I declared to God I would never trust Him. As a young man, it was unconceivable to me that He didn't answer her final prayer to allow her to live so she could be with her family. I had never told a single person of that time in my closet. Nor did I tell anyone of the oath I had uttered in my grief.

This woman described that closet and my statements in exact detail. She went on to tell me that the call of God on my life required me to deal with that moment and my oath. Interestingly enough, this woman would have been about the same age as my mother. Once she had finished speaking to me, she stuck out her hand to pray for me, placing her hand on my head and closing her eyes. Looking back, I realized that I hadn't shed a tear from the moment I made that declaration in the closet to that moment standing next to the woman praying for me. That would be about ten years.

Side note: I never considered myself a crier. I am a byproduct of my father, who I only saw cry once in my life. My stoicism is ever-present to this day, unless I have one of my grandchildren in my arms. Other than that, much to the chagrin of my wife, I rarely show emotion. Certainly, in public it was unthinkable to shed tears, but in that moment, as she laid hands on me, I made up for 10 years of it.

I have never felt so overwhelmed by God's love for me as I did that day. God took down all my walls, and invaded my soul to bring the healing to me that I needed more than my next breath. What had become acceptable to me was unacceptable to God. It wasn't that He was mad at me or even disappointed, He was acting in love to bring me to a place my oath had kept me from. From that moment forward, I have had no trouble with prayer, worship, or connecting with God, and my relationship with God has never again been an issue.

In addressing our call to be a fighter and a warrior for God's kingdom we cannot overlook the personal need to have something addressed internally that may deeply affect our ability to follow God's directions. In the book of Jeremiah, after God called him to prophesy to a sinful and unrepentant people, God told Jeremiah something that stands to this day as God's equation to make us effective for His work.

Jeremiah 1:10 reads, "See, I have this day set you over the nations and over the kingdoms, to root out and to pull down, to destroy and to throw down, to build and to plant."

Notice that God told Jeremiah to do four seemingly negative things before He would do anything positive. Notice that to turn Israel from their idolatrous ways, deep measures would have to be undertaken.

To *root out* meant that the sin could not be dealt with on the surface. The term *pull down* meant that what was built out of rebellion must be taken from the view of those who had erected it. To *destroy* and *throw down* meant that every semblance of structure standing in the way of God was to be obliterated. It was only after these four actions had been done that God could do the positive in His people: build and plant.

Before we as individuals can be truly effective in the fight, we will have to submit to God to deal with what may hinder us. In my case, the oath I made in my closet would have become a great hindrance to His plan for my life. Paul, in his attempts to teach the church to stay in the fight told them to cast down every imagination and every high thing that exalted itself against the knowledge of God.

In other words, Paul is saying we are to deal violently with anything coming into our heads that goes against what God thinks about us. We cannot ignore our own mindset and the issues that can hinder us. There is a reason why the military requires every single recruit to go through a selection process. Boot Camp is designed to strip down everything that can hinder that young person from being effective on the battlefield. But it is not only designed to strip down, it is designed to equip and empower. Yet before the positive can be placed in the heart of a soldier the negative weaknesses have to be fixed.

Both Jeremiah and Paul are telling us the same thing: Don't allow your mind to get into the way of God's plan and don't allow your experiences to define your future. Years ago, I remember a big deal in some churches over the issue of something called inner healing. This was the practice of healing traumatic memories, sexual abuse, and many other issues hindering attempts to serve God.

Personally, since I had experienced a deep inner healing myself, I was very open to it. However, in time I developed some deep reservations as I saw people go to serious extremes in its exercise. At one point I was tempted to throw the idea out altogether. As I searched the Word of God and my own heart, I couldn't discount God's commitment to the healing of the mind and soul. Jesus is not only the healer of the body He is the healer of the whole man.

To have any other concept of God minimizes the work of Christ's death on the cross toward making us whole.

Several years ago, I remember sitting down with several recently rescued sex trafficking victims and the person protecting them. To say that each of them was in deep pain is at best, an understatement. The youngest was maybe 11 and the oldest 14. As we spoke, I remember almost having a panic attack at the thought that I had nothing to give them to help their pain. I mean, what do I know of the pain of the brutality forced on them?

To be used again and again on a daily basis and to endure the terror of their captors was something I could not even begin to comprehend. I don't totally understand why I reacted this way but I did. It wasn't long before I realized what I had to help them with was an introduction to the Great Physician, Jesus Christ.

You need to know that in order for you to live as a warrior and ultimately find a good death, Jesus is all the help you need. Nothing in your life is outside of His ability and willingness to heal. Once Christ plants in you a new vision of yourself, you become the capable warrior dressed and ready for battle to do the work of the kingdom of God.

The Fight Against Fear

"But in all these things we overwhelmingly conquer through Him who loved us." Romans 8:37.

Fear is one of the largest obstacles in the way of God's plan for our lives. In fact, the enemy effectively uses this tool to keep us in from experiencing the life God wants us to live.

It stymies our growth as a person and causes us to accept fear imposed restrictions thereby limiting our potential.

When we find ourselves at this point, truth which challenges our limitations is the only answer to our forward movement. God's word is truth. Not just some of it, all of it. One passage which has broken insecurity and fear over my life hundreds of times is Psalm 139:23-24. "Search me, God, and know my heart; test me and know my anxious thoughts. See if there is any offensive way in me, and lead me in the way everlasting." This is David's invitation to God to search him. That request took guts! David is telling God that he is unwilling to allow his own judgment of himself to define his actions. He asked God to challenge him in every corner of his heart and soul. The person who practices this will undoubtedly become the fullest expression of his or her purpose in this life. I have a promise for you. If you can muster up the guts to follow David's example, you will meet a God who is more than you ever imagined. As a result, you will see yourself doing things you formerly considered inconceivable.

Fear of intimacy with God

God wants to get closer to us than perhaps we are comfortable with. It is fear which convinces us that this is acceptable. Many of us are subconsciously unwilling to get too close due to lies which hide in fear. Even though we know that the sacrifice of Christ has given us a green light to be intimate with God, we still would rather keep Him in the distance. This is dangerous because it can become the breeding ground for a religious spirit. All dead religion has one thing in common. It places something between God and man. If we were brutally honest with ourselves, we would have to admit that we like it that way. Because we fear the result of God in our space we worry that God will make us do something we are afraid of. That He will embarrass us, and shake up all of the "safe places" we run to when we feel insecure.

If these sound familiar, then you are among the majority of Christians today who would rather do the minimum to maintain faith than to press into the deep place which Christ bought with the greatest sacrifice ever known among men. Please don't take that as a judgement, but rather, as a challenge. Let me ask you, do you want to squeak into heaven dragging all your fears like a child drags an old blanket, or do you want to arrive to the sound of His voice, saying "well done?" It is your choice and I hope this admonishment pushes you to become great in Christ.

I've noticed that that when a person gets closer to me than arm's length something changes in me. Because they have entered my space without permission I react negatively. The first time I entered a church, a stranger approached me and attempted to hug me. I backed away and slid past her quickly pushing my way into the door. Offended, I thought, what was that crazy person doing? At the time, I had a serious issue with people getting in my space. I soon realized that this carried over to my relationship with God.

I am sure like me, you have met people who cannot communicate without touching you and getting closer than arms distance. Most of us have a visceral reaction to this kind of interaction. When this happens. suddenly I am not hearing what they are saying, but rather I am focused on other things. For instance, I will hold my breath and become over concerned with my personal hygiene. Truth is, I want to choose who gets to be in my space. Now let's look at how this can become a problem with intimacy with God.

God will only draw close in intimacy with those who want Him. That is not to say that there aren't times when He chooses to overwhelm us with His touch. But intimacy is a shared experience between willing parties. With Jesus, He is always willing. His door is never closed. Even when we are soiled by sin and shame, He has made a way for us to come to Him. The question is, do we? Intimacy isn't supposed to be a rare experience, but rather the standard in our relationship with Jesus.

We cannot become the warrior God intended us unless we are revealed. Christ's intimacy causes us to see ourselves for who we really are. Out of love, He exposes our fears, unbelief, and sin. Distance doesn't define us, intimacy is the only way.

There is a reason why a drill instructor gets in your face when he is turning you into a warrior. It is because what is instilled while he is in your space changes you. It is the same with God. He hated the idea that He could only be close to us through the veil of the temple and its priest. Which is why the first thing that happened when Christ said it is finished and died, was the ripping of the curtain in the temple, signifying the end of a distance between God and His people.

Sometimes I like to make a point using a play on words. For instance, the word "intimacy." To best understand how this works with God and us, it is helpful to see that word like this: in-to-me-see. When we ask, and welcome the Father to see into us, the response God always gives is, in-to Me-see. Intimacy is an exchange. It is never one way. But for us to receive all that we need to be a good warrior and effective servant, we must get over this fear of intimacy.

The Bible tells us that the prophet Isaiah was minding his own business one day when God decided to show up and get very personal with him. God decided to get in his space. Because Isaiah's mind and imagination were yielded to the Lord, the Lord was able to give Isaiah a full Technicolor, Dolby-sound vision of Himself. This vision was so awesome that it caused Isaiah to fall to his knee trembling.

Suddenly finding the presence of God in his life quite intimidating and threatening, he cried out, "Woe is me, for I am ruined!" Isn't that an interesting response from a mighty man of God? God comes to him, and he feels ruined. In effect, it's as if he is saying, "God that's too close; please don't get that familiar. I don't want to give you access to see into me."

Friend, remember this: to the degree that you allow God to see into you, God will allow you to see into Him.

Psalm 139 says, "Lord, you have searched me and you have known me." Christians who want to experience freedom in Christ will embrace God's intrusion into their lives, but those who resist will be like Isaiah who hid his face before God and said, "Woe is me!" Interestingly, after Isaiah said this, he admitted what God was gently pointing out, "Lord I am a man of unclean lips."

I find Isaiah's struggle with God interesting. You see when God got close to him the source of Isaiah's sin was exposed, resulting in his heartfelt confession. The source of his sin is much the same as many of us, his lips or the words which were coming out of his mouth. Fear rose up in him in this amazing encounter with God, and out of his mouth came the words, "Woe is me." If this is where the story ended it would be tragic. For many of us whom God confronts with our sin this is where it stops. There is something in us which cannot accept a God of forgiveness. That fallen nature still wants judgement and once we feel the guilt of our sin we end the encounter there.

But God, in response to Isaiah's acceptance of responsibility essentially said, Isaiah, I didn't draw near to you to make you grovel but to get close to you so we could fellowship. I've come alongside in order to help you deal with those issues which are keeping you from the fullest expression of your purpose in life.

Then the Lord sent an angel with tongs, and touch the source of Isaiah's sin thereby cleansing him so he can arise from his guilt and fellowship with Me.

God wants to enter our space so He can first expose what we're laboring under and then heal us. In doing so, He restores the intimacy every believer should have with Him. You see, our God will never convict us of our sin just to make us squirm. On the contrary, God's conviction is one of the greatest gifts he has ever given us because with His conviction always comes the means to repentance and total restoration. When we sense the conviction of God, remember it is His act of love to us because He wants to draw you into closer intimacy with Him. He wants to show more of Himself to you.

Today, the relationship you have with God is your choice. If I choose to deny God access to my space then for the most part He will. The result is I will know about God but will not know Him as an active participant in my daily life.

At the beginning of every New Year, I ask myself a question. Greg, if you knew you couldn't fail this year, what would you do? Then I write down those ideas, dreams, and goals. It is interesting what happens once I have written them. While they remain in my head they are easy to ignore. But once I write them they become faith goals of which I am steward over. As the evolution continues, a conflict begins in my mind and doubt begins to knock at my door. Fear produces those "what if's" and amplifies the temptation to abandon the dream altogether. I have just described spiritual warfare. Your identity in Christ, destiny, personal calling, and relationship with God, are directly related to the dreams God births in you. Evil fears the one who faces it, and presses toward what the bible calls the "high calling."

Surrounded

Today I am deeply concerned at the rising rate of suicide. Each year 44,193 Americans die by suicide. In my lifetime, I have never seen so many people who feel such hopelessness that they take their own life. The other day I was talking with several of my adult children and this subject came up. I was baffled as each of them told me of the huge number of their high school friends and acquaintances who had either died from suicide or drug, specifically opiate and heroin overdoses. If I were to identify one factor which is present in all suicides, it is the feeling of being surrounded. To be specific, this is the feeling that there is no light, no hope, and the pain will never go away. This is the case for those with the disease of addiction or those suffering from Post-Traumatic stress, either from war or a traumatic event. Or depression which so many good people suffer from. Each of these emotional diseases is as much a cancer to a person as if they have a physiological cancer. This begs the question, so then what is the answer? There is a story on the bible which underscores something we must have today.

In the book of second Chronicles chapter 20, the bible tells us of a king named Jehoshaphat. The king was faced with an enemy who was coming to steal his inheritance. We are told that while the King was in his palace a messenger came to him and said, "King Jehoshaphat, and army is amassing against you." He was surrounded. As could be expected the king was afraid. There is nothing wrong about being afraid especially when we feel surrounded. It is a natural human response to an attack. It becomes wrong when we stay that way. What the king did after feeling afraid can save a life. The Bible tells us that in response to his fear, he initiated three strategic actions. First, he turned his attention to seek the Lord. When we feel surrounded no matter what the cause, our survival functions click in to either fight or flight. Suicide, or even the consideration of it, is a flight response. For those reading this who have considered such an act please don't take this as a criticism. We are all made of flesh and bone. We all have extenuating circumstances which form our psyche and emotions. There is nothing wrong with the flight response unless you follow it. In turning to God, Jehoshaphat gives us a valuable weapon in the fight against suicide. It is the knowledge that we cannot face being surrounded alone. We need help! Also, that help is not far off. No matter how bad things look to us, Jesus is always right there. He is the One who promises to never leave or forsake us. Secondly, Jehoshaphat proclaimed a fast throughout Judea. This tactic is so powerful when it comes to hopelessness and depression. He allowed others to share his pain and sacrificed his control over the situation. Fasting is the act of denying self. Suicide is the ultimate act of control over life. In this desperate act, the suffering shuts out God and every other living being. By proclaiming a fast Jehoshaphat allowed others to both share the pain and help to come up with an answer. Thirdly, the king gathered the people to seek help from the Lord. I cannot overstate the importance of this last action demonstrated by the King and his people. The power of agreement in those times when we are surrounded can make the difference between life or death. This is exactly why Jesus established the church. Because it is the place where we can gather with others who have the same faith, and agree in prayer to stand and fight.

No matter what you are facing at this moment, take heart that you are not alone. Regardless of what your surrounding enemy is saying, you are a valuable and loved child of God. He loves you more than you could ever imagine. Never let that truth go. Never!

2 Chronicles 20:6 "Lord, the God of our ancestors, are you not the God who is in heaven? You rule over all the kingdoms of the nations. Power and might are in your hand, and no one can withstand you."

David or Saul

As we examine fear another story in the bible speaks volumes about both the power of fear and the power of faith. Most of us have heard the story of David and Goliath. In my many trips to Israel, I have had the pleasure of standing in the very spot that battle took place. On one side of the valley were the armies of King Saul and the Israelites and on the other the Philistines and their spokesman Goliath. This giant of a man was an expert at eliciting fear in others. In fact, his demeanor alone was a weapon. But the Philistines understood the paralyzing power of fear. Even though the army of Israel was militarily more powerful and experienced than the Philistines, the sight and sound of Goliath caused them to collectively seize up.

As a leader, Saul failed both God and his army by allowing more than two words to come out of the mouth of that bloviating bastard of a giant.

1 Samuel 17:11, On hearing the Philistine's words, Saul and all the Israelites were dismayed and terrified. This was game over for Israel unless a true warrior arrived on scene.

Somewhere near this spectacle there stood a young man named David. For the most part he was treated by his family with mild neglect. He was given the task to shepherd the sheep and this day, while tending them, he was asked to take them supplies. Fast forward to David's arrival at the battle. As he arrives on one side of the valley he sees his many brothers along with their king Saul and the rest of the army standing with their heads down and their weapons in the dirt. On the other side of the valley he sees the Philistines and Goliath shouting his threats. I Samuel 17: 26, "David asked the men standing near him, "What will be done for the man who kills this Philistine and removes this disgrace from Israel? Who is this uncircumcised Philistine that he should defy the armies of the living God?"

This shows us the correct response to the intimidations that are often thrown in our path. We need to have a major problem when words are used against us in the attempt to keep us from progressing. Through David, God is teaching us that no matter how big and ugly the intimidating force is arrayed against us it only takes a little faith and a lot of attitude to overcome.

CHAPTER 10

CARING FOR THE WOUNDED

"War drew us from our homeland. In the sunlit springtime of our youth. Those who did not come back alive remain in perpetual springtime—forever young—and a part of them is with us always."

Author Unknown

"Never shall I fail my comrades. I will always keep myself mentally alert, physically strong, and morally straight. And I will shoulder more than my share of the task whatever it may be, 100% and then some."

Ranger code:

It is impossible to talk about war and warriors and ignore the reality of the wounded. It is an unfortunate fact of war that there will be casualties. To make matters more challenging spiritual warfare is not a battle that is fought fairly. Our enemy has a fortified and well tested system that has a great track record of taking out those who have had the courage to stand and fight. To suggest that our Christian heritage is a promise of a life without wounds is nothing short of heresy. There is no doubt that engagement in God's fight will have consequences that are not pretty. To willingly see the ugliness of war, spiritual or otherwise, will cause us pain.

Over the past several years, I have traveled to many war zones and sites of terrorism. Some of them have had a deep impact on me, as I will never forget the sights and sounds I experienced. Some of my trips stand out. For example, I first visited Ukraine during the revolution in 2014. Our team spent days in the rubble surrounded by death. According to the Huffington Post more than 6,000 people perished in this conflict. Many of those men and women died from snipers shooting very high caliber ammunition that cannot be stopped by a normal helmet or armor. Basically, the people demonstrating on those streets were sitting ducks to the vicious snipers.

I vividly remember a number of experiences I had while there. One day as we walked through the maze of tents, tires, and sandbag I found a helmet laying in some bushes. My curiosity got the best of me and I picked it up. When I examined it I realized that there was a bullet hole and blood in it. After replacing it to where I found I shuddered at the realization of what I had been holding. A man was murdered wearing that helmet just days before I arrived. All because he was fighting for freedom. I still remember the smells of death, and the wailing of old women and grown men. Since that 2014 trip I have traveled back to the Ukraine two more times. During each trip, I cannot fight off the past. I accept it as a scar and part of the life I am supposed to live.

On another trip, I was asked to go to Nepal right after the devastating 7.8 earthquake that took the lives of 9,000 people and demolished more than half a million homes, most of them in rural areas cut off from emergency care. During that trip, we flew helicopter missions into cut off villages to provide urgent care. I cannot adequately describe the utter devastation we saw. Mountains just buried hundreds alive and erased any sign of life in seconds. In the city, people lived in tents because they were afraid to occupy their homes in the fear that they too would be buried alive in an after-quake event.

We heard that a United States Marine chopper went down, killing all six marines. The unit that those marines were from was set up right next to where our supply helicopters were. I remember observing the remaining marines busily tearing down their camp. They had been ordered to dismantle the camp. They had their heads down and were obviously devastated at the death of their friends the night before. I prayed with several of them and offered the little counsel I could before they departed.

These are just a few of the stories of my personal experiences. I regret none of them, and embrace whatever mental or spiritual scars that are a result. History has taught us that the sights and sounds of combat can leave those who experienced it incapacitated in "normal" life. The memories of what happened have the potential of rendering those involved almost incapable of lasting happiness if not dealt with appropriately. This condition not only affects the one who personally know the trauma of war, but also those surrounding them. However, we can overcome this condition through communication, open discussion, and reframing of the soul.

While great strides are being made in dealing with the mental aspect of war, often the spiritual ramifications are left undealt with. In many discussions, I have had with those who know first hand the ugliness of war, it has become clear that there is often a lingering struggle with guilt and feelings of unworthiness with God. I call this post-combat spiritual stress. This condition causes one to think that a previously active and vibrant faith and closeness to God is no longer possible due to the activity of war. Because war in some manner involves the possibility of taking another's life, there is often a lingering doubt in the soldier's mind as to how God may view his or her actions. Questions concerning the morality of war and the validation of the actions of those who fight it can result in spiritual confusion and lifelong separation from God.

Healing for this condition requires a reframing of the soul and spirit through the exchange of the soldier's human perspective for God's divine one. There is an interesting passage from the Old Testament that helps explain this reframing. Jeremiah 29:11 (NKJV) says, "For I know the thoughts that I think toward you, says the LORD, thoughts of peace and not of evil, to give you a future and a hope. Then you will call upon Me and go and pray to Me, and I will listen to you."

Because of God's omnipresent divine nature, He is able to keep all of us in mind at the same time. In fellowship, the Father is completely present in the moment to each one of us in a deep and intimate disclosure. To those suffering from post-combat stress, that kind of close relationship is often avoided due to post combat guilt and self-imposed condemnation. This is especially true when there is a lingering doubt regarding the morality of one's actions on a battlefield.

Recently, I counseled a sailor serving in the Special Forces. He had just returned home from extended combat duty in Iraq and Afghanistan and was deeply troubled about his relationship with God. In our conversations, he disclosed some of the details of his actions in battle along with the questions regarding how he could reconcile his experiences in his relationship with God. It was during that time that I realized the need for scriptural clarity on the issue of how God sees the soldier post-combat.

When a soldier takes another man's life, regardless of how just the killing was, it changes him or her forever. This is especially true when that soldier, airman, marine, or sailor is a Christian, having known God's presence and goodness and having developed a conscience softened by the Holy Spirit. It makes him question how God sees him and if the wrong conclusions are reached, the resulting distance in relationship has tragic ramifications. Real or false guilt negatively affects fellowship with

God. Therefore, it is vital to spiritual health that they are dealt with appropriately.

The first thing that must be dealt with in the quest for spiritual health is to determine if the guilt is real or false. If the guilt is the result of sin it must be repented of and then turned from. If the guilt is false it must be renounced and overcome. Today there is much being said about the difference between murder and killing. There is no doubt that murder is forbidden in Scripture.

Killing is often condoned and encouraged when dealing with those considered enemies of God. In the world of war and combat the lines between killing and murder often get blurred. It is understandable when the believing soldier comes home from a deployment confused about how God sees his or her actions. It is in these cases that one must look at how God dealt with his servants when they were guilty of murder.

For instance, in Exodus 2:11, Moses murdered an Egyptian man and then buried him in the sand. Then again in 2 Samuel 11, David was guilty of murdering Uriah. In both cases, the murderer was God's called and anointed servant. In each case, while the man reaped pain for his actions he was not saddled with debilitating guilt and separation from God for the rest of his life.

This shows us something about the heart of God in the matter of human failure. Our God is forgiving and He has demonstrated a desire that nothing would separate us from His love. Especially today, because of the sacrifice of Christ, no excuse exists for the believer to maintain any distance from God. As Hebrews 4:16 reminds us, "Let us therefore come boldly unto the throne of grace, that we may obtain mercy, and find grace to help in time of need."

One of the most powerful tools for restoring God's desired fellowship with us is the knowledge of God's perspective of our lives. Because of the work of the cross, the Father has made the conscious decision to see the good in us. When Jesus gave His life on the cross, He became our advocate with the Father and because of His sacrifice, the Father now looks upon us differently. Because of Christ, the Father doesn't see us through our experiences of war, our failures, or our personal lacks but rather through the righteousness of Jesus Christ.

Many believing soldiers are stifled in reaching their destiny because they have embraced the multiple-layered lies of the enemy. When their minds are constantly occupied trying to sort out the dark thoughts and feelings that accompany duty, God's perspective is often ignored. Jeremiah 29:11 gives a clear message that in order for progress in God's order of things the soldier MUST make a connection with the Father's genuine thoughts toward him, exchanging all other thoughtful consideration in the process.

The devil is a liar! He is a master at finding ways to get into our heads with misrepresentations of God's true perspective of our lives. On a daily basis, he is actively communicating lies to God's people regarding how God views us. As such, we must always be on watch for the lies that will be thrown at us. The devil's motivation is simple: to alienate us from God and estrange us from His thoughts toward us. The tragedy here is this: We cannot get to where God wants us to go until we make a connection with what He is truly thinking about us. The lies we embrace cause us to stall in our spiritual growth. Paraphrased, I read Jeremiah this way: "WHERE I WANT TO TAKE YOU REQUIRES THAT YOU CONNECT WITH MY THOUGHTS TOWARD YOU."

The Holy Spirit wants us to be better at taking down the strongholds of lies and deceit that reside in our soul. If we are truly going to be God's agent in the fight of faith we must become adept at this activity. The devil's goal is simple: to keep us from the source of God's power. The minute we identify with God's true thoughts toward us, we are emboldened with the greatest source of power one can experience in life. It is God's desire that we make the connection every day with His mindset toward ourselves, toward others, and toward our surroundings.

Almost everything in life has a voice. Our hurts and pains each have a voice. Our fears and insecurities each have a voice. Our past experiences have a voice. And certainly, our circumstances have a voice. Since each voice can communicate both good and evil, whichever one you listen to most will determine your quality of life. Scripture says that there is constantly a battle going on in our lives between the flesh and the spirit. Practically speaking, this means that the voice of the flesh and the voice of the spirit are always competing for dominance.

At any given moment, God is trying to get through the chatter of the voices of the flesh in order to speak truth to our soul and spirit. Often, I wonder if God isn't shouting, "Will you please STOP the chatter and JUST LISTEN TO ME? You've been trying to do it yourself and it hasn't worked. You've been trying to save your marriage and it hasn't worked. You've been trying to fix your financial dilemma and it hasn't worked. You have been trying to deal with the memories and images of combat and it hasn't worked. Maybe it's time you just STOP TRYING TO FIX IT YOURSELF AND LISTEN."

Our happiness and success depends upon how quickly we find and renounce the voices that are not of God and replace them with God's perspective. The apostle Paul had more reason than most to walk around in guilt. Before accepting Christ, he did all of sorts of evil things—including participating in murder—that could have tormented him when he was trying to proclaim the message of Christ. One can only imagine what could have been going through Paul's mind as he represented Christ to a lost world.

Let me ask you something? What happens to you when you attempt to tell people about Jesus? If you are like most people the immediate memory of your last sin or your lack of prayer and Bible reading comes into your head. It doesn't take a genius to see the reason why. The devil doesn't want you to share your faith or the name of Jesus. The devil doesn't want you to be doing the things God's called you to do. He knows how to attack you in those moments when you are about to change another's life.

Because Paul was susceptible to guilt, it is no wonder why God gave him the following passage. Second Corinthians 10:5 (KJV) reads, "Casting down imaginations, and every high thing that exalts itself against the knowledge of God, and bringing into captivity every thought to the obedience of Christ." Here, Paul is showing us how to do spiritual warfare against the lies that often fill our heads. Whenever God is misrepresented, it must be dealt with through determined spiritual warfare. Paul tells us to "cast down the vain imagination that exalts itself against the knowledge of God." In other words, we are to violently deal with anything that comes into our mind that is inconsistent with what God thinks about us.

In order for us to adequately do this we must first KNOW what God thinks. Paul said, "Cast down every vain lying imagination." What is imagination? An imagination begins with an image. If the image is not dealt with immediately, it becomes an imagination. When the imagination is not dealt with, it soon becomes a stronghold. Once a stronghold takes hold in our mind, the result is separation. This is a perfect definition of post-combat spiritual stress.

In order for you to be successful, you must become adept in doing this kind of spiritual warfare against lying images. Falsehood doesn't just go away or fade over time. It must be aggressively addressed in spiritual warfare by imposing God's mind over the lie. When it is not possible for that to be accomplished alone, we must enlist the help of others to bring down this darkness.

Today, more and more Christians are accepting distant, cerebral relationships with God devoid of His power because of the presence of falsehood in the soul. It is an act of spiritual warfare to press into God until there is an exchange made, God's thoughts toward us for the lie.

One of the reasons why so many Christians today are inept and unable to bear fruit is because they haven't done what Paul said with the lies that are floating around their heads. Let's face it, not one of us deserved what Jesus did on the cross for us. He died for us while we were yet sinners. But God still chose to love us and gave us access to His Kingdom both here and in eternity. When Christians walk around in guilt and maintain a distance from God it grieves the Father because it ignores His grace and the powerful redeeming work of the cross.

There is simply no reason for us to walk around in guilt. We are to approach God each day to cleanse our hearts and minds. We are admonished to confess our sins and forgive others. This is the act of spiritual warfare enabling us to continue to run the race that is set before us. When this is successfully done for our entire life we will reach the end of our days and hear those glorious words, "Well done, thou good and faithful servant!"

To be successful as a believer, you have to identify and empower God's thoughts regardless of your circumstances in life. This is especially true for those who are called to serve in the military world as well as others who are engaged in God's fight where emotional and physical pain is commonplace. I have often wondered how the martyrs could sing praises while being tortured and burned alive. Their pain must have been excruciating but in the midst of their agony they apparently found something that enabled them beyond human abilities.

I believe that in their moment of sacrifice, they connected with God's thoughts, which brought nothing but praises out of them. Instead of screaming in agony, they shouted in praise, because something supernatural happens when we connect with what God is thinking. In the worst of their situation, they identified and activated God's thoughts over the moment. They were rewarded by a good death and then everlasting life.

As Philippians 4:8 (NKJV) states, "Finally, brethren, whatever things are true, whatever things are noble, whatever things are just, whatever things are pure, whatever things are lovely, whatever things are of good report, if there is any virtue and if there is anything praiseworthy—meditate on these things."

It is clear in Scripture that our quality of life will directly follow what we allow to fill our minds. Therefore, we are duty bound to keep our minds in the best condition we are able regardless of circumstances. I have referred to Jeremiah 29 several times because it has such great relevance to almost any situation we may find ourselves in due to our acceptance of God's fight.

Jeremiah 29 is written to captives living in the worst possible conditions. Yet God has nothing but good to say to them. It says a great deal about the attitude God has about circumstances controlling us that He tells them to build houses, marry and give in marriage, and build and plant during their captivity. Our captivity has absolutely no affect on His vision for us. Our individual excuses as to why we do not engage in His plan for our lives are not important to God. We all have problems and many of those problems are very tragic. But we cannot expect God to excuse us from duty simply because we have problems.

All humans will go through seasons where we will wonder if God really cares about us. That is especially true for those serving in combat in a distant land where death and destruction are everywhere. Sometimes we become so overwhelmed with our outside surroundings we allow them to become the definer of our life. We enclose ourselves in what we convince ourselves is a legitimate hiding place. While I am convinced that God compassionately understands, there still remains no hiding place but in His presence. Since we cannot avoid difficult times then we have no option but to deal with them according to His plan and will, which is to run to Him and rest in His presence and love.

Maybe you just returned home from a deployment and you are struggling with your role in battle. Or you may be the lonely spouse of someone on deployment and you are dealing with all the pressures of life alone. Maybe you are hanging in there, but you are about at the end of your rope. You may be wondering when it is all going to end. The answer is, the moment you connect with God's thoughts about your life.

Wherever you are in life, whatever your surroundings, however good or difficult life may be, God is saying, "I want you to prosper in your captivity." Furthermore, He said to the people while captive, "I want you to build and plant gardens." Sometimes the last thing we want to do when we're going through a rough time is focus on something productive. But the Lord is saying, "If you're looking through what I think about you, you will build and plant. You will marry and you will have kids. You will bear fruit regardless of your circumstances."

Beyond that, He even said, "I want you to seek to prosper in the city of your captivity." Scripture is full of examples of men and women connecting with God's thoughts and seeing their circumstances change, but my favorite is in the story of Joseph. In Genesis 37 Scripture says Joseph dreamed a dream. After speaking that dream, he was promptly thrown in a pit and sold into slavery. Then, just when things started going good again for Joseph, Potiphar's wife lied about him and he was once again placed in captivity.

But Joseph couldn't be stopped because wherever he was in life he connected with God's thoughts toward him. The result is clear: Every place he was put only served to lead him to the fulfillment of his vision. God's promise is this: "My thoughts are the key to prosperity and the means to freedom ultimately."

Here are four points that will help you embrace God's thoughts: First, don't give your captivity your devotion and your meditation. Open the Word of God and praise God. When you begin to praise God, you begin to connect to the thoughts of God. God knows how to meet the need if you REFUSE to allow it to consume you.

Second, do not entertain the voice of your captivity. A movie was recently released about the life of Louis Silvie Zamperini. It is called "Unbroken." It tells the story of how this amazing man refused to allow his captivity to define who he was and how he thought. Louis served as a bombardier in B-24 Liberators in the Pacific. On a search and rescue mission, mechanical difficulties forced Zamperini's plane to crash.

Louis, along with two others, drifted at sea for 47 days until he was captured by the Japanese, who occupied the Marshall Islands. He was taken to a prison camp in Japan where he was brutally tortured and starved for two years. Following the war, he initially struggled to overcome his ordeal until he turned to Christ to help him forgive his captors.

What are you going through today? Has it defined you? Are your walls closing in on you? I promise you that if you rise in rebellion against your tormentors God will meet you there. You will rise up in strength and blow down those walls.

Third, enlist the power of God to deal with your captors. Until you forgive them, you are linked to them, and that's the worst possible thing that could happen. Forgiveness is one of the greatest weapons we have available. It goes contrary to logic and the natural human response to those who have hurt us. But when we forgive, we are emulating what Christ did as He faced his good death. "Father forgive them for they know not what they do," are the words of a warrior refusing to allow his torturers to define Him.

Fourth, declare that your captivity will end on God's terms, not your captor's. God gets the final word. That assures a good death. Because I want you to see the practical way this works, I will share the following real life story of Jason. Because of our ministry, to the military we often receive letters from our troops asking for help dealing with the leftovers of their valiant service. The following is one of them.

Dear sir,

I need prayer for my PTSD issues from Iraq. I am embarrassed to admit it. I only have issues when fireworks go off and some other things. I hate it that I live down the street from a church and they shoot off big fireworks, every 1st of January and 4th of July. I was a supply guy in an infantry battalion, Fort Carson, Colorado. I also need prayer for my walk with the Lord. I fail a lot and I feel depressed. I don't feel that folks, including some of my family, understand how it was in Iraq. I've never been so scared in my life. I was there 2008 to 2009. We had to sleep and do our business with one eye open at all times. I hate having the panic attacks when I hear loud fireworks and having to hide in my closet, trying to make excuses when my wife and 5-year-old son see me balling my eyes out. My wife tells me that I'm no longer in Iraq. I tell her, YES, but Iraq is in me. My mom said the Lord told her that my problem is soul wounds. I don't know exactly what that means. Can you help me?

Thank you,

Jason

This is our response:

Hello Jason,

I am glad you contacted us. After reading your letter, I would like to thank your mother for her insight in suggesting you have a soul wound. She may be correct in respect to what you may be suffering. A soul wound is a type of moral injury. Christians and many other religions understand the meaning of a person's immortal soul. It is the part of a person that lives on after their physical death. While a person lives, their soul, regardless of their religion, begins to form from birth. It is that part of a person known as their soul—their mind, their spirit, and their way of thinking— that we view as their moral integrity. It is also a part of a person as susceptible to injury as any part of the body. The military is just beginning to understand that moral injuries can be just as harmful as physical injuries. For a long time, moral injuries have been viewed as psychological injuries, such as PTSD. Many times, trauma is treated as a deficiency in a person's ability to think clearly. While most psychologists and psychotherapists do excellent work in helping sufferers of trauma, not everyone suffers from just mental injury. The main difference we are finding between psychological and moral injury is that moral injury is not a problem with how people think but rather what people believe. From birth we build our belief systems of "good and bad," "right and wrong," "likes and dislikes," and especially "us versus them." On these building blocks we create our world, family, friends, work, etc. War as you have seen has a tendency of changing all of that in the most traumatic way. Those beliefs that we have held to be true for so long are suddenly NOT true or so it seems. For example, fireworks to most people involve a time for celebration. For you this is no longer true. Those loud noises are your reminder of combat. The army over decades of trial and error has learned how to create efficient training programs for the purpose of taking ordinary civilians and creating disciplined fighting men and women. We are trained to act in response to our surroundings without a need for too much reasoning. As you know in combat, if you have to think about your response your chances of being injured or even killed goes up. During your deployment(s) in Iraq, you may have experienced the need for this rapid response. You also may have seen firsthand that even when soldiers do everything right, it's not enough to save them from harm. There is a certain helplessness that comes with this knowledge. I don't know whether or not this is the case with you, but some people begin to question whether or not any of their beliefs are true. Sometimes, certain things such as a smell, or a picture, or a loud noise triggers a chain reaction that puts them right back into this train of thought. As an example, the fireworks may, in an instant, take you from reacting to a firefight, then realizing that you are no longer in theater, to remembering the helplessness you felt, to how can you help your own family. I know this is a lot to consider and some of this may not apply to you at all. However please remember, the fact that you can think means you have a good start on recovering. Think about what you believe, especially those people and things you love. Remember that you are good at many things but not everything. No one is good at everything. Some things you just won't be able to fix. When that happens, find help. Even in the military, we depended on each other to get the job done. It's the same here. Your memories from Iraq will not just disappear, but over time you can put them in an order which matches your view of the world as you knew it and create a world that works for you. Lastly, everyone has a very unique way of seeing the world around them and so do you. Your knowledge, your understanding, and your experiences (good ones and bad ones) make you unique. We care about you as an individual and a huge contributor to this nation. Even though I don't know you personally, I pray the Holy Spirit helps you see the benefit of all your qualities and strengths and helps you find support for every weakness. In some respects, your wife is also going through a form of trauma as well. The wide-eyed husband full of life and hope for the future is not the man that returned to her. Her "just get over it" comments are common and come from those who don't understand what many in the military go through or why they changed. It's okay, as given time and your support she can learn to love and respect the new you. Together you can renew old loves, find new ones, rekindle hopes and dreams, and together make them come to pass. Thank your family and friends for their support and don't be afraid to contact the VA crisis helpline if you would like to speak with someone in your area. Don't hesitate to write or call me as well. By the way, not everyone likes fireworks, guns, or loud noises and that's okay too.

Your friend,

Greg

We are God's only hope for the world. Christians bear the mark of Christ on their heart. It is because of this that we must stay in the fight. But also, we must have answers for those who have been wounded. When our answers are born of God's wisdom they will have a deep effect on those who are hurting. Many of the warriors who will fight the most valiantly have yet to be saved. But is it through those who have once hurt and have come to Christ for help that we become the agents Jesus can use to hear warriors and establish them in the battle for the souls of man.

Christ and His Wounds

Scars are obviously the result of wounds. I am one who believes that every believer enters heaven the same way the Lord Jesus did, with wounds. While our wounds are not in the same category as Christ's, they are nonetheless proof of battle and reveal the hits we took, whether while we were in the fight or while we were avoiding the fight. I find it intriguing that Jesus ascended into heaven in his perfect body WITH HIS WOUNDS. One would think that His new body would be devoid of the markings of His suffering but instead He took His wounds with Him into eternity. I asked myself why? And the only answer I could come up with is that the wounds were a badge of honor in heaven. Is it too much of a leap to think that the wounds we experience while doing His will on earth will also be a badge of honor? To all those who have suffered in the line of duty as a believer and to all those who are still suffering, that revelation is vital. It is not wrong to be wounded, it is a testimony of courage.

There are some similarities between natural warfare and spiritual warfare. One similarity is that wounds are not always caused by the enemy. Sometimes we are wounded by "friendly fire." That term seems an oxymoron because friendly fire it isn't! There are also wounds caused during training, wounds caused preparing for battle, and then wounds caused by our own stupidity. Regardless, if the wounds are caused in the process of serving God's cause then they are all badges of honor.

CHAPTER 11

EIGHTEEN DELTA

n Special Operations, there is a unique group of men who have earned the designation of "18 Delta" medics. This man is the doctor of his platoon and is the most highly trained battlefield lifesaver in the military. The lifesaver of the unit is not your average medic. The Special Forces medic employs the latest in field medical technology and limited surgical procedures. He is capable of managing any battlefield trauma injury, as well as administering preventative medicine.

The special operator medic is an integral part of civic action programs in bringing medical treatment to native populations. These medics also become paramedics upon completion of their medical training. Their capabilities include advanced trauma life support, limited surgery, dentistry, and even veterinarian procedures. Each can train, advise, or lead indigenous combat forces up to company size. I bring up these kinds of people because I believe we live in a time where we are going to need men and women who are trained for the traumas that are prevalent in our day.

We need "18 Delta" believers who can respond to the carnage on the battlefield of faith. Vietnam veterans did not have a distinction yet called PTSD. So, they suffered without help for decades. In a scary way, the church is where the Vietnam veterans were. Since we do not address what I call post-traumatic spiritual disorder yet, we are leaving our wounded on the battlefield. The following underscores my claim: Hundreds of pastors leave the ministry each month due to moral failure, spiritual burnout, or contention in their church. Thousands of new churches begin each year, but more churches will close. Fifty percent of pastors' marriages will end in divorce. Seventy percent of pastors constantly fight depression. Eighty percent of seminary and Bible school graduates who enter the ministry will leave the ministry within the first five years. Ninety percent said the ministry was completely different than they thought it would be before they entered it. Seventy percent felt God called them to pastoral ministry before their ministry began, but after three years of ministry, only fifty percent still felt called.

Ministry Today reports the divorce rate up 279% in the last twenty-seven years. An ABC broadcast reports that the divorce rate in the Bible Belt is fifty percent higher than in other areas of the country. The Barna Research Group reported in January 2000 that twenty-one percent of atheists and agnostics will or have experienced divorce, while twenty-nine percent of Baptists and thirty-four percent of non-denominational Christians will or have experienced divorce. The average rate for all Christian groups is twenty-seven percent.

These stats are the result of a church without a sufficient plan for taking care of its wounded. These are catastrophic figures and tell only one story about our ability to care for and rehabilitate those who have been wounded, some severely, while engaged in the fight against the enemy of our soul. They underscore the fact that our present day theology doesn't give priority to building men and women who are trained and proven in the process of restoring those who have fallen.

Note that while we are adept at producing counseling for those who have "normal" problems associated with life, there is a major difference in counseling one who has fallen while in the fight, then counseling those who are not. For instance, spiritual warfare produces abnormal association with the demonic. This confrontation causes what I referred to earlier as post-traumatic spiritual disorder.

In a 2009 article for *Christianity Today* magazine, author Jocelyn Green gave readers a glimpse into the lives of different military officers suffering from post-traumatic stress disorder—with special attention given to the responsibility the church has in ministering to those officers. She writes:

Nate Self's military record was impeccable. A West Point graduate, he led an elite Army Ranger outfit and established himself as a war hero in March 2002 for his leadership during a 15-hour ambush firefight in Afghanistan. The battle resulted in a Silver Star, a Purple Heart, and a position as President Bush's guest of honor for the 2003 State of the Union. But by late 2004, Self had walked away from the Army. In another surprise attack, post-traumatic stress disorder (PTSD) had taken his life captive. "I just hated myself," says Self. "I felt like I was somebody different. And since I didn't feel like I could be who I was before, and hated who I was now, I just wanted to kill the new person. I felt like I had messed up everything in my life. The easiest way, the most cowardly way to escape, was to just depart.

Those who suffer from PTSD continue to react, sometimes more intensely than ever, to a traumatic or life-threatening event even after the danger is past. The main symptoms include troubling memories and nightmares, hyper-vigilance, depression and anxiety, emotional detachment, and avoidance of crowds or anything associated with the event. The symptoms often lead to substance abuse, chronic unemployment, and homelessness. Two out of three marriages in which one spouse has PTSD fail. The suicide rate among those with PTSD is almost twice the national average. Suicides were up in all the armed services in 2008, with 125 confirmed suicides in the Army alone—the most the Army has seen since it started keeping records. Since PTSD wasn't officially recognized until 1980, many of today's veterans carry scars from not being properly cared for upon coming home from previous wars.

In 1970, after 14 months in Vietnam, James Knudsen returned as a decorated combat veteran. A Christian and regular churchgoer, he has suffered from PTSD ever since, resulting in long-term unemployment, severe depression, and a failed marriage. John Blehm also returned from war in 1970, but wasn't diagnosed with PTSD until 27 years later. "Before then, people just thought I was a crazy alcoholic," he says. Today, Blehm and his wife, Karen, teach classes at Skyway Church in Goodyear, Arizona, for those with PTSD and their family members. The nondenominational church offers professional counseling at an affordable price on its campus, at the Window to Healing Center. Skyway's approach represents a positive and growing trend among U.S. churches in addressing PTSD—a change that's been a long time coming. "The church dropped the ball on our generation," says Vietnam vet and PTSD sufferer Frank Vozenilek. "We cannot afford to drop the ball on this one." Today, Vozenilek and Knudsen assist churches in the Cedar Rapids/Marion, Iowa, area in meeting the needs of veterans with PTSD.

Retired U.S. Navy SEAL Mark Waddell says his church was "absolutely oblivious" to his family's desperation when he was dealing with PTSD, but that a fellow member, Sue McMillin, offered very practical help: she spent seven hours helping him clear his garage, which was full of boxes of military gear left untouched since Mark had returned from combat in Iraq. "Mark could not bring himself to open the bags and boxes because of the weight of the memories," says his wife, Marshelé Carter Waddell. "He was avoiding all the triggers that lurked inside—sand and dirt from the desert, mud and blood on his boots. So, the garage continued to be a negative thing in his life. With Sue's help, we hauled away a truck bed full of paraphernalia and clothing, and reorganized and labeled all the plastic tubs." "Mark went through the memories and the triggers with us by his side, with people who love him and want him to heal, who didn't allow him to stop and walk away. It was very difficult for all of us, but at the end of the day, Mark's load was lightened dramatically."

The church has also played a critical role in Nate Self's healing. Though Self was involved in a PTSD small group at Veterans Affairs, it was his … small group that proved most beneficial. Though some of his PTSD symptoms remain, they are much less severe. He now works as a consultant on officer-training materials for the Army, and is active in First Baptist Church's military ministry, which serves more than 100 military families in its 3,500-member congregation. "If people think the VA hospital will solve all the problems, they'll overlook the greatest source of healing in any situation: Jesus," says Self. "The majority component for recovery is a spiritual solution, more than any secular clinical answer."

The importance of people stepping up to accept the call to be spiritual medics who are adept at bringing healing to the wounded cannot be overstated. I have a dear friend who is my hero in this area. I have known Michael Cook for more than twenty-five years. He is one of the finest men I have ever met and one who I would consider an 18 Delta spiritual medic. Michael flew a medivac in Vietnam.

Daniel Tyler describes being a medivac pilot as landing your helicopter at a crossroads in the middle of a rubber plantation near the Vietnam-Cambodian border to pick up a wounded South Vietnamese soldier who's been stitched across the chest with four machine gun rounds. It's listening over the intercom to the door gunners guiding you down into the little "hover-hole" and knowing that the North Vietnamese are hiding just down the road in at least two directions with you in the sights of their AK-47s. It's watching the patient jostle and bounce like a sack full of apples as four members of his rifle squad run out and throw him onto the floor of the helicopter and then dive for cover.

Michael became a pastor and counselor and to this day has never stopped picking up the wounded from the battlefield. He is one of the most gifted men I know in the area of healing the soul and spirit.

Early one Saturday morning in San Diego, I was invited to attend the inaugural meeting of the Life of Valor men's conferences hosted by my close friend and former Navy SEAL, Jeff Bramstedt. It was an all-day event with several speakers, including Jeff, and amazing music. There were about 400 men in attendance. The purpose of the event was to call men to pick up their weapons and live again as God intended, as warriors.

I have known Jeff for more than a decade and he served our nation in the SEAL teams for more than 14 years. During the years I have known him, he has been a brilliant and gifted man. Beyond his military career, he has acted in at least 30 major motion pictures, and is an accomplished musician, a mentor of young men wanting to follow his path into the SEALs, and an amazing father. He is a man's man!

The problem is he was wounded from the many difficult experiences he endured both in and out of military service. That day, Jeff was speaking like I had never heard him speak. He was transparent and open about his life, including the resistance to get help for his wounds. Even after repeated exhortations, Jeff was a typical warrior who believes they can take care of everything themselves, treating their own wounds.

But after a divorce and continued devastating experiences, Jeff finally humbled himself and went to see Michael. That day in

San Diego Jeff told the story of three days of agony with Michael as the Holy Spirit moved to heal him. He told the story of how God opened him up, removing the emotional and spiritual shrapnel, resulting in the miracle of healing and peace.

Today, Jeff continues to do greater and greater things in this world as a healed soul. Michael is a warrior. But he is also a medic. With the gift of healing and mercy, the Holy Spirit uses him time and time again to bring wholeness to those who have given up hope. If you were to meet Michael, you would never identify him as a warrior. This underscores the truth that it isn't the outside that marks a warrior. It is the gifts of the spirit that make a warrior.

All of us have been given special gifts by the Holy Spirit. And when we are acting in those gifts we are functioning perfectly as a warrior, regardless of what is revealed on the outside. Many times, those with gifts like mercy and healing are often not the type A people. They demonstrate a less demonstrative visage. Usually, these people are the Michaels of the church; believe me, when you are wounded, they are the most valuable people you can find.

Caring for Those Morally Wounded

Young and full of faith, a husband and his young spouse make the decision to enter into the ministry because they really believe they can make a difference in the lives of those God has called them to. He begins some sort of educational pursuit and she supports him as best as she can with all the stress of the lack of finances along with the care of kids. His hours are long in study and when the subject comes up that there is a lack of intimacy or quality time spent together the common response is, "The mission is worth it." Yet that is where it begins! Not only are the seeds of ministry being planted into the heart of this young couple with all the theological training needed to be sent out into the world in Christ's name, but also the seeds of something diabolical.

In all my years working in ministry I have never met someone entering into God's service that was not completely pure in their desires and motives for entering it. The passion and the vision were there to do great things for God and unless something catastrophic happened the promise of a great life serving God was easy to foresee. Now, decades later I find that many of those I watched enter into the fight right, have fallen.

More often than not some sort of sin was a major factor in the fall. It is important to note that all humans are made to need affection, especially those who are constantly giving through ministry. This means that all humans are vulnerable to the possibility of having that need met immorally. There is no doubt that sexual sin is not in a decline among believers.

Statistics show that it is one of the most prevalent sins men and women are bound by in and out of the church today. This virus has spiritual roots and represents the front lines in the battle for forward motion in the church. It is taboo for us to speak about it much in the church, especially among leaders. For the most part there is an expectation placed on leadership in the body of Christ to rise above these kinds of sins simply because they are leaders. I am well aware of the scriptural admonition that requires purity as a prerequisite for spiritual leadership but what is the plan when a leader begins to fall into the trap of the ages of sexual sin?

Harry W. Schaumburg, the executive director of Stone Gate Resources, a ministry pointing people away from sexual sin, states the following:

"Christians are in deep trouble and anyone who doubts that is spiritually asleep (1 Thessalonians 5:6). To understand the breadth and depth of this crisis in the church we must have the courage to look inside. The problem is not the pornography on the Internet or the many opportunities for sexual sin in our sexually saturated culture. It is the potential for wickedness in our own hearts coupled with the secrecy of our personal lives. The critical questions to ask are: Is my personal life shaped by my beliefs, ideals, and traditions as it once was? Is my faith effectively shaping my integrity as a Christian? Do my beliefs make a difference in my private sexual life?

There is a loud silence that must be pierced before the real problem of sexual sin will be understood and dealt with. We can start on the surface with the all too common examples, but we must also go to the unseen depths of the human heart. In humility, ask the Spirit of God to search your mind, look behind your closed doors, and examine the recesses of your heart.

The following documents true accounts of tragedies which take place when we refuse to examine our heart. When researching for such accounts, there were so many but I chose just enough to make the point.

1. Driven by lust and sexual fantasy, a pastor and his wife engage in threesome sex with their 20-year-old nanny. The pastor rationalizes his behavior by citing the multiple wives of biblical characters.

2. For years a young man corrupts his mind with sexual fantasies. He eventually has sexual relations with three underage girls and goes to prison.

3. A father of three, married for 19 years, has a 17-year affair with his secretary, who is his wife's best friend. For years, they vowed to God and to each other to end the relationship before it destroyed everyone in their lives. A young wife leaves her husband and two children to work in a strip club.

4. The wife who feels lonely and abandoned finds comfort in the arms of another man."

We must heed the words of Paul: "Brothers, if anyone is caught in any transgression, you who are spiritual should restore him in a spirit of gentleness. Keep watch on yourself, lest you too be tempted" (Galatians 6:1). There will be no grief or gentleness until we see the deceitfulness of the human heart, the deceitfulness in our own hearts, and dig the log out of their own eyes. Then the Church can begin to adequately address the pervasive plague of sexual sin.

Schaumburg goes on to write: "The biblical standards of human sexuality may not be easily accepted by new converts or maintained by Christian couples that have grown up in the church. The problem is not simply a weakened attitude toward sexual sin or the minimizing of sexual sin, but a failure to know the real enemy. We must be trained to fight this war and know the enemy within. We cannot know another person's heart, but deceitfulness keeps people from facing the truth of who they are inside. An examination of the darkness and ignorance in one's heart should not be avoided. A look at indwelling sin is humiliating and takes courage and wisdom, but if believers have any interest in pleasing the Lord, knowing His will (Ephesians 5:10,17), and avoiding sinful behavior that grieves the Holy Spirit (Ephesians 4:30), they must accept this challenge."

Make no mistake, sexual sin has taken out more great warriors than any other weapon. This is exactly why we need medics who use their gifts to free those taken out by it.

Caring for Those Wounded by Disillusionment

One of the most debilitating wounds I can think of is the wound of disillusionment. This is a wound that comes when a man or woman looks back and regrets what they see. It comes when the lie enters the soul that says it was all worth nothing.

Jack (not his real name) is a dear friend and someone who I always considered as a peer; a man I always wanted to emulate.

We had many things in common: both pastors of churches, both mentored by the same man of God, and both fathers of large families who over the years vacationed together many times. He was successful for most of the years I knew him when suddenly about five years ago I began to see a dark change.

He would make statements to me like, "I just don't feel much life anymore!" or "I just wish I were single and lived alone!" I must admit that I didn't know exactly how to respond when he said these things and I certainly didn't recognize that he was disillusioned with just about everything. He even began to question whether God wanted to have anything to do with him anymore. Then his world began to crumble!

It started with the dismantling of all that he had spent his life building. His church crumbled before his eyes, the land he bought to build his dream home on was taken over by an unscrupulous land developer, he was fired from the board governing the project he intended to be his legacy, his home was foreclosed upon, and he finally filed for divorce from his wife of more than 25 years.

Many today wonder how such a great man of God could wind up like this. But in all that has been said about Jack, I have found few who really knew the truth. Jack was wounded by disillusionment! Once that wound is inflicted the infection sets in and the rest is history. The real tragedy in all this is that no one, including me, had any idea how to help Jack through his pain. Instead, men judged, men cast stones, and men unknowingly helped the process of his demise. I have since come to realize that if there were enough people who knew the signs of disillusionment, much, if not all, of his downfall may have been averted.

The problem today is we do not have much of a medivac plan for those who are wounded in spiritual warfare. When someone has lost hope in an area they have always been strong, there needs to be a plan for getting that person off the front lines into a place of care. Furthermore, the church needs to allow for its leaders to experience such episodes and account for this in their expectations. These are those who are wounded warriors. They are not out of the battle, they are just wounded from it.

Many years ago I was involved in a movement that embraced something called inner healing. Wikipedia describes inner healing this way: "The Inner Healing Movement refers to a grassroots counseling movement among Christians of various denominations. Its principal method is calling up suppressed or hurtful memories in order to deal with them." This movement for the most part was made up of people whose heart was in the right place.

They recognized the need for healing beyond what was obvious. I was a recipient of that type of healing more than once. Then over time, people began to misuse the gift. They began to use the vulnerable conditions among those they were counseling to control and manipulate them. Soon, many evangelicals began to say that this practice was heretical and was all a sham. Inner healing as a term and practice became anathema.

Over the centuries this has been the typical practice of the church. If there's some type of error, instead of fixing it they throw out the whole thing. The problem is that many who were used by the Holy Spirit to bring inner healing to others were gifted by God to do so. And now they are in spiritual hiding. The conditions in our world today require that the healers and counselors come forth once again.

Learning from the mistakes made in the past, we move on. We need to once again open the triage centers needed for the wounded warriors of God. When we are wounded, the church is the first place we should be able to find help. But, if the church as an institution is unwilling to accept that call, then those willing must heed the call to find the wounded, and restore them to fitness.

CHAPTER 12

THE BATTLEGROUND

"True religion confronts earth with heaven and brings eternity to bear upon time. The messenger of Christ, though he speaks from God, must also, as the Quakers used to say, "speak to the condition" of his hearers; otherwise he will speak a language known only to himself. His message must be not only timeless but timely. He must speak to his own generation."

Knowledge of the Holy, A.W. Tozer

Manhood is in serious trouble today. The confusion among males regarding what the true meaning of manhood is has not been so difficult to find since the times of Sodom and Gomorrah. There is no hope for men today unless males join the fight. If we don't join the fight the fight will surely join us. The only problem is we will be the defeated instead of the defeaters. We simply must stop treating men like sheep, but instead lead them like warriors. No more swords presented in ceremonies suggesting manhood achieved. Let's leave this kind of show to the movies. No more acting like warriors with no intention or courage to actually battle and bleed. No more talking heads in conventions where we tell men how to be a man of God, without any lasting challenge.

Make no mistake about it, this generation is waiting to hear the battle cry of our day. And when they hear it, there will be a rumble of boots following that cry into the heat of confrontation with darkness. Many cannot even see the war that is raging right under their very nose. And that is because they don't want to. I am one who believes that strong, moral men are the backbone of any health society. Conversely, when the men of a society are weak or weakened, then the society will follow.

A revealing piece on psychologytoday.com called "The Demise of Guys" by Philip G. Zimbardo and Nikita Duncan illuminates the very issue I am talking about here:

"Everyone knows a young man who is struggling. Maybe he's under-motivated in school, has emotional disturbances, doesn't get along with others, has few real friends or no girlfriends, or is in a gang. He may even be in prison. Maybe he's your son or relative. Maybe he's you. In record numbers, guys are flaming out academically, wiping out socially with girls, and failing sexually with women.

Asking what's wrong with these young men or why they aren't motivated the same way guys used to be isn't the right question. Young men are motivated, just not the way other people want them to be. Society wants guys to be upstanding, proactive citizens who take responsibility for themselves and who work with others to improve their communities and nation as a whole.

The irony is that society is not giving the support, means, or places for these young men to even be motivated or interested in aspiring to these things. In fact, society—from politics to the media to the classroom to our very own families—is a major contributor to this demise because they are inhibiting guys' intellectual, creative, and social abilities right from the start.

Consequently, many guys lack purposeful direction and basic social skills. They're living off, and often with, their parents well into their 20s and even 30s, expanding their childhood into an age once reserved for starting a family and making a career. Many young men who do manage to find a mate feel entitled to do nothing to add substance to that relationship beyond just showing up. New emasculating terms such as man-child and moodle (man-poodle) have emerged to describe men who haven't matured emotionally or are otherwise incapable of taking care of themselves.

Hollywood also has caught on to this awkward bunch of dudes, who appear to be tragically hopeless. Recent films such as *Knocked Up*, *Failure to Launch*, and *Hall Pass* present men as expendable commodities, living only for mindless fun and intricate but never realized plans to get laid. Their female co-stars, meanwhile, are often attractive, focused, and mature, with success-oriented agendas guiding their lives.

The sense of being entitled to have things without having to work hard for them—attributed to one's male nature—runs counter to the Protestant work ethic, as well as to the Vince Lombardi victory creed ("Winning isn't everything. It's the only thing."). These guys aren't interested in maintaining long-term romantic relationships, marriage, fatherhood, and being the head of their own family. Many have come to prefer the company of men over women, and they live to escape the so-called real world and readily slip into alternative worlds for stimulation. More and more they're living in other worlds that exclude girls, or any direct social interaction, for that matter.

Over the past decade, this pattern has escalated into adulthood where grown men remain like little boys, having difficulty relating to women as equals, friends, partners, intimates, or even as cherished wives. We believe this demise can be traced to the rise of technology enchantment. From the earliest ages, guys are seduced into excessive and mostly isolated viewing and involvement with texting, tweeting, blogging, chatting, emailing, and watching sports on televisions or computers. Most of all, though, they're burying themselves in video games and in getting off on all-pervasive online pornography.

We are focusing primarily on guys investing too much time and energy in the last two factors: playing video games and watching freely available Internet porn. Video game production companies are in fierce competition to make games that are ever more enticing, more provocative and, now, in 3-D. The same is true for pornography. Pornography is the fastest-growing global business, with production companies churning out daily doses of porn flicks in seemingly endless variety. The high-definition 3-D porn wave may also be coming (pun intended). The combination of excessive video game playing and pornography viewing is becoming addictive for a lot of guys. The next phase we imagine is transferring the player's viewpoint onto the body of the protagonist to mesh realities and make digital environments totally egocentric.

There are also other factors contributing to the demise of guys: widespread fatherlessness and changing family dynamics, media influences, environmentally generated physiological changes that decrease testosterone and increase estrogen, the problematic economy and also the dramatic rise of gals."

It used to be common that when boys didn't pull their weight they were made to feel ashamed. Whether that meant to work hard on the farm, join and fight in the military, or place themselves in academics, to become a productive part of society was expected. Now we are inventing "acceptable terms" to describe men who are unwilling to become a man.

This is not a time for men to hide behind those terms. It is time for the boy who should be a man to come out of the closet. Tom Brokaw wrote a brilliant book called *The Greatest Generation*, which was about the men and women who lived through two world wars. One of the reasons he called them the greatest generation is because they lived like they were in war, because they were. They lived a life of sacrifice and gave their all to deal with tyrants, despots, and murderers. My mentor and hero is the late Dr. Edwin Lewis Cole. He was the master of one-liners affectionately called "Colism's." One of the greatest phrases he ever uttered was, "being a male is a matter of birth, but being a man is a matter of choice."

If we soon do not have a move of God among men who call themselves Christians, we are going to be overrun and defeated. If the men of God do not stop allowing themselves to be browbeat by a feminized society that demands equality at the expense of real manhood we are doomed. I do not care if I am called names for what I believe.

Just because I do not accept a male acting like or turning himself into a female or a female acting like or turning herself into a male does not make me "phobic." In fact, I have yet to meet someone living that lifestyle that had the slightest capacity to elicit fear in me. If I offend others because I am unwilling to shut up when injustice is looking me in the face, then too bad. I am not afraid of weak men or a weak society.

My faith tells me I have a responsibility to fight it. Confrontation, whether or not it is intended for me or coming from me, is a part of being a real man of God. I don't judge a man for chewing tobacco, drinking a beer, or uttering a word that is not commonly accepted, because that is what warriors are like. I would rather be around a guy who chews tobacco and drinks a beer than with a metrosexual who is carrying a purse.

Warriors do not mind dust, mud, and the smells of sweat and blood. They are willing to do whatever needs to be done to win, even if it costs them everything. They do not give up on the man fighting next to them, ever! Today, the reason most men do not know a war is raging around them is because they are so busy fighting the war going on in their own soul that they spend the majority of their lives belly gazing. If we cannot win the war inside of us, we will never know the real war and the real enemy.

A real man is a person who holds TRUTH to be his most precious possession. It is that TRUTH that he lives out in his life and hands down to his children and their children. What is acceptable in society has no bearing on what is acceptable to me. Political pressure, well...isn't! When a politician dies for me, making a way into eternal life, then I may at least talk about it but until that happens my faith is the director of my life.

A man loves his family with passion. He protects them with everything he has. He sets a standard and refuses to move from it no matter what others say. He accepts the fact that sinners will act like sinners and he can hang with those who are exceedingly gifted at sinning and not judge them or change to be like them. He is a living epistle, a walking message of strength through good times and especially in bad times.

A man walks through life like a soldier walks through the streets of a war zone. He has eyes in the back of his head, his head on a swivel, always vigilant, always ready, always training, always putting his body and soul under pressure so it is not foreign to him when real pressure shows up. He is never too old and is not out of the fight until the Lord takes him home.

Macho bravado? Chauvinistic ramblings? Call it what you want but that is the truth in my book. By the way, I intend to respectfully prove Mr. Brokaw wrong. The greatest generation is yet to come. Hopefully it is not too late for an even greater one to arise.

The Mission

So, what is the mission? I can tell you what it is NOT. It isn't about looking to starry constellations and blood moons. This is foolishness. It isn't about buying and hiding food and money. It isn't about fear of God's judgment on the nation. If anything, that's already happened with the rise of our corrupt government and the deluge of God-hating, demonic voices filling our airwaves daily. I would think that if God is looking for a nation to judge He could find a whole bunch of other nations more evil than America to level. (I will resist the temptation to make any suggestions.)

But we are still a nation of righteousness and hope because there are men and women like you and me in it to stay His judgment. If you and I are true to our calling, then our mission is to love what God loves, hate what God hates, and war against the things that misrepresent Jesus' true nature. If I learned anything in my numerous trips to war zones, disaster areas, and riots it is that we are never supposed to be out of the fight. The BEST place for us to be is in the fight, among those suffering, and wounded, and hungry for the true God.

The battlefield is where our lives of faith can carry the ONLY hope available to this world. With this mindset, some of us may take a hit or two as the enemy fires at us, but the heart of the warrior stays with us whether conscious or not. God is moving among His people to reveal what has been hidden deep within us. Our desire has come to the boiling point, as we realize that it is time to represent the spirit of the coming Lord, riding on a white horse with a sword raised.

The enemy has attempted to silence the most valuable prophetic voices of this hour. It has not worked, and it is because all of us are God's voice now. We have a duty to carry on the mission and to declare defeat to the enemy by speaking God's heart. We carry the sword and are called to run toward the battle and fight as our mentor has taught us. That is the mission! On the mountain of transfiguration, a Voice came from heaven and said: "Hear Him." Our mission is to hear, and then boldly and in faith to declare. As my SEAL friends would say, follow your orders and shoot, move, and communicate.

There is something in every man that seeks to be part of something bigger then himself. Even if he denies it, there will always be a nagging feeling to rise above selfish pursuits to achieve the mission. The best way for me to communicate the essence of mission is to draw from the military culture. A mission is not just a fly-by-night thing. A mission comes from the head shed, (command or control center), as a directive. It gives specifics regarding every aspect of the planned event. Those orders are then given to those capable of carrying out that specific mission. Those tasked with its completion then jock up, man up, deploy, and complete the task.

In a religious world, it is always tempting to etherealize things. That is to say we make things so spiritual that there really isn't any clarity or urgency attached to what is said. The problem with this is Jesus was not into giving us a bunch of suggestions. When He told us to go into all the world, He was giving us a mission.

Contrary to common belief, that mission was not any different from the military mission I described above. There is no question that each male reading this has a mission or missions we will answer to God for. At the end of our lives on earth, either we will have completed our mission on earth or not. In case you are wondering what yours is, here is a wonderful quote by Frederick Buechner: "The place where God calls you is the place where your deep gladness and the world's deep hunger meet."

It is easy to make mistakes once we begin our pursuit of God-ordered mission. Because so many things around Christian circles are called "missions" we can easily just go with the flow and do whatever others say. But like most things, all that is presently called a mission has nothing to do with what God considered one.

The truth is most people really don't know what a mission is, and so they let others, including church mission directors or commercials of emaciated kids, motivate them. In my recent world travels throughout war-torn disaster areas I can tell you first hand that there are many missions important to God that are not even on the grid of most Christian leaders or churches.

It is absolutely true that Jesus called us to go into the world and preach the gospel. That broad command has an application according to the call God has placed on us individually, but it must be emphasized that none of us are left out of the general call to be God's voice to the lost and hurting.

Society as a whole will produce more and more pain because it is under the control of the god of this world. Satan cannot produce anything but pain for fallen men. Since those who have come to faith in Christ have to live in that society, we often are touched by the pain and suffering. But we have to remember that even Christ didn't automatically reach out to the suffering while He was on this earth. He underscored this when He said, "I only do what the Father tells me."

In other words, society doesn't dictate to me where I go or what I do. Only the Father has that right. Through church history individuals have stepped forward, putting into practice what the church as a whole has always said it believed. These godly individuals have led the way establishing hospitals, orphanages, schools for the poor, and places of refuge for the outcasts of society. Without those who sense a calling and step forward to lead, compassion becomes merely a theological position in the church—faith without works that is dead.

Those called by God to take on the social and moral challenges of their generation are not always cheered or supported by Christians and the church. Their sense of clarity and willingness to get into inconvenient and sometimes dangerous situations make believers very uncomfortable, especially those who are less clear about moral challenges and less willing to get involved.

It isn't that difficult to identify where the war is both in the natural or the spiritual. All one must do is simply ask the question, what does God love most? It may sound overly simplistic but Satan exists to destroy what God loves. For example, if I wanted to know how much God loves children all I would have to do is look at the enormity of what has been done in the past 60 years with abortion and now with child trafficking.

My connection to the cause of child sexual slavery began in the former communist-ruled nation of Romania. I traveled there to help a friend conduct a large men's meeting consisting of several hundred executives attempting to come out from under the mindset and the limitations of a former communistic ruler. It was a wonderful trip as I was privileged to be front and center to observe men come out of their shell and become innovators and free thinkers.

One night after our meeting, I was asked to dinner with several federal officers involved in the country's fight against human trafficking. During dinner, the head of the human trafficking unit began to tell me about the huge number of children who were being trafficked from Romania and other Eastern bloc countries to other nations where they were sold into prostitution, some as young as three years old.

I was aghast as I listened to the stories of disappearing children and the large numbers of families who had been devastated by the unthinkable. The dinner lasted an hour or so and as we said our goodbyes the lead officer placed a thumb drive in my hand with the comment, "When you get a chance please look this over!"

While on the airplane home I settled into my business class seat, a novelty made possible by my traveling companions' miles, and I felt like a monarch with my own video screen, a reclining seat so I could sleep, and the excellent service provided by the American Airlines flight attendants. I think I was about an hour into the flight when I was startled by the voice of God. He said, "I am not where many think I am, but I am with EVERY ONE of those children."

That moment marked the end to my comfort on that flight as I began to ask God what this statement meant. Until then, I considered the meeting as another interesting conversation and didn't give it much more thought until the moment when God spoke that phrase to me. As most around me were sleeping I pulled out that thumb drive and watched the video. It underscored the unbelievable pain and torture these children were enduring and with it came a startling understanding that this was not just some rare thing but it was part of the second largest criminal enterprise on earth today: human trafficking.

After watching that video, I closed my computer and began to ask many questions. Why would God speak to me about this? What can I do about the problem? Then it struck me that God NEVER speaks a word to anyone just to speak it. Every word God speaks to the heart of a man has an attachment that essentially enlists that man into a service or activity of some kind. For me that means His word to me on that airplane enlisted me into a new battle, one that would take my life in a direction I would have never dreamed.

After I arrived home I continued to pray about what happened and the burden to DO SOMETHING grew and grew until I realized that I had spent a decade working with those who had the unique skill sets to go after the very core of the unspeakable evil of child sexual slavery. Think of it: The SEALs and Special Forces personnel all have to retire at some point.

Most of them are in their very early 40's when they do retire, which means that they are not only young enough for a new task outside the military structure but would be more than willing to continue to use their skill sets in this kind of mission. Each of them has spent the better part of twenty years honing the skill of investigating, capturing, and eliminating those who bring terror to the hearts of the innocent. I remember thinking, what if we could build an organization with these men with a mission to legally investigate pedophiles and give the completed cases to the officials who would prosecute and imprison them?

Over the years, I had developed a deep friendship with a former SEAL who I found particularly unique. He was a godly, moral man still married to his wife of several decades, a great father to his daughter, and a brutal but poised, seasoned warrior. He had spent the bulk of his Special Forces career serving in clandestine operations supporting the efforts to eradicate despots and terrorists. One day I called him and recounted to him the story of Romania and it didn't take long for me to realize that he was the right guy to call.

Since I had no experience at all in the operational side of things it soon became clear that my friend was the guy to build the team of men to hunt down those who are responsible for the terrorism of the innocent of this world. In only a couple of calls we came up with a plan that was only lacking one thing, the money to fund it. Later that week, I flew to Dallas where I was asked to speak at a pastor's conference. While I was speaking, I mentioned my experience in Romania and exhorted the pastors to be more active in issues of social justice.

After I closed, a well-known pastor and his wife almost tackled me as I walked toward the exit. They said, "We've got to talk!" We stepped outside away from the crowds and it soon became clear that this man and his wife were in the same place as I was. God had spoken to them about the same time I was in Romania and told them to begin a walk across America designed to raise awareness about child trafficking and raise money to fund the work of those who would hunt down predators.

His dilemma was that he had no idea how to find people who were able to hunt those responsible for this horrendous evil. In that moment, we knew that all the pieces were now in place. To fully understand this situation, some facts need to be known. One of the leading experts in human trafficking and a former Bush administration official said: "We must show new strength in fighting back an old evil. Nearly two centuries after the abolition of the transatlantic slave trade, and more than a century after slavery was officially ended, the trade in human beings for any purpose must not be allowed to thrive. The new human rights movement to end trafficking in persons continues to gain momentum."

It is my personal belief that this fight for justice will, in many different forms, invade the consciousness of many believers. When the people of God take up the cause of justice for those who cannot fight for themselves they are entering into one of the most unique forms of spiritual warfare. It is important to know that if you are closed to the issues of justice, then you are closed to God, because God has always been linked to the issues of justice.

This is not just a fight against those who are guilty of this abuse but it is a battle against the spiritual forces who are behind it. It is important to note that the very physical action of social justice is an act of war against the demonic forces that are feeding the lust of evil men. The church needs to know that while it is essential to pray against these kinds of things, prayer without action is incomplete spiritual warfare. Complete spiritual warfare involves both the spiritual component along with the natural component.

Justice is foremost in the heart of the Lord Jesus today for the church. I believe the church's involvement and acceptance in this cause will usher in the next spiritual movement, revival, or whatever you want to call the tangible presence of Jesus among meeting believers.

According to *Relevant* magazine, "[The year] 2014—will go down in history as having the highest level of global persecution of Christians in the modern era. The worst thing, though, is conditions suggest this is only going to worsen around the world in many areas where Christians face a lot of persecution."

We cannot simply stand by and do nothing when our brothers are being murdered for their faith. We must fight back by any means possible. And that means entering into the fray and being willing to lay down our lives if need be to fight this evil. When I say fight, I am referring to all things necessary from every source available. This includes, but is not limited to, manpower, finances, training, education, and open discussion among believers worldwide. Time, talent, and treasure are needed. Remember, the Lamb finished His role. Now the Lion (Christ) is the Spirit who leads us.

The Old Fight and the New Fight

There is a term used in the military today called the "rules of engagement." These ROE's usually only help the enemy, because they are determined by political concerns and do not take into account the grey of war. Because the enemy only has one objective—which is to steal, kill, and destroy—fighting against such an enemy cannot be done by tying warriors to a one-sided restriction. The good news for Christians is the ROE's given from Christ do not keep us from exercising justice on the devil or his imps, rather they empower us to take our authority from Christ and dispense holy justice.

There is no question that we are all called to fight the fight of faith. This is not just some ethereal, pie in the sky, objective. We are called to defend, fight, and win. We are called to set those who are captives free from their captivity, and if need be, eliminate those who stand in the way.

Today, the most popular books and movies are those that depict justice against those who have done unthinkable things against the innocent. There is a reason for that. It is because all sane men hate those who prey on the vulnerable. And the vulnerable love those who prey on the ruthless. In fact, even felons doing time in prison hate those who prey on children. When the opportunity arises, even the felons dole out prison justice. When others act in a manner that brings fear on the innocent, the righteous are obliged to act, and the act is not to seek a truce. A truce only serves to leave a fire lit in the enemy, only to be revealed in another moment. Peace can only come through victory.

There is certainly a great value to apologetics, which is the defending of the message of our Christian faith. The question I pose in this book is this: Is giving verbal defense enough when confronted with life and death situations? If someone doesn't want to hear, what do we do then?

We are to expose falsehood, including doctrines that make a way for Christians to believe wrongly. One example of this is seen in the argument that Christians worship the same God as Muslims. In this book, I will not give much detail on the danger of such a false teaching, except to say that this belief is patently false. In fact, it is akin to making an alliance with our sworn enemy. Islam and the Koran hold all Christians as infidels and as such are worthy of death. There is not a single correlation between the false teachings of Islam and those of Jesus Christ. To believe that Allah and the godhead of the Bible are the same is to bow to the devil himself.

There can be no alliance with the devil or his false religions. Every Christian has a responsibility to defy the false teachings of Islam and to defend those who are brought under the slavery it brings upon all who believe the Koran. The brutality that Islam brings upon its own believers should turn the stomach of any truly saved Christian. If that brutality is acceptable to the teachings of the Koran, one can only imagine what brutality is acceptable to the infidel, which is anyone who believes anything other than Mohammad taught.

It is true, that as an individual, you cannot fight everything. It can be overwhelming at times, with all the suffering and wrongs being perpetrated on others on a daily basis, to know our individual role. So, I recommend that the best place to start is to realize that God has not placed you on this earth without the calling and ability to be a part of this fight. This acknowledgment is the first step.

Next, ask yourself what makes you feel alive. The writer of Hebrews wrote: "Therefore, since the promise of entering his rest still stands, let us be careful that none of you be found to have fallen short of it." Each of us has something unique and God-given to contribute to this life. Regardless of how you feel right now, that fact remains true. You, yes you, are of worth. Finding that unique gift is what makes this life exciting.

Gil Bailie said, "Don't ask yourself what the world needs. Ask yourself what makes you come alive, and go do that, because what the world needs is people who have come alive." The other day, I was with several doctors who are experts in treating addictions and post-traumatic stress disorder. When I was told the statistics of men who are addicted to opioids today, I was stunned.

I realized that addiction is the ultimate surrender and renders one useless in God's cause. It is capitulation to hopelessness. Addiction comes when we don't feel alive. When we don't spend time with things that bring us life, we fill that void with destructive substances and unhealthy relationships. We have a promise, one given by the Lord Himself. It is a promise of His rest, and His rest is defined as the mindset of peace that arises from one who has found why he is alive.

You will not feel more alive than when you are engaged in the fight you were born for. Conversely, you will not feel more dead than when you are not treading the ground of your warfare. Your fight will find you if you are looking for it. But this knowledge comes with a caution. Our fight is not against the church or our brothers in Christ.

Regardless of the right or wrong we see in the church, that fight is not for you unless you can be a productive and positive part of instituting change. We don't need critical, negative people who think it is their God-given right to be critical. Also, our fight isn't to judge God's people. That right is for Him alone. This book is called *A Good Death* for a reason. A good death cannot be achieved by someone with a critical or judgmental spirit. Internal fighting isn't a fight sanctioned by God. In fact, a fight between brothers is not a fight at all.

Instead it is strife, which the Bible tells us opens the door to every kind of evil. This is not to say that God will not use you to bring correction to other brothers. Correction done as an act of love, whether or not it is received, should be typical to Christian relationships. A good death is achieved when we fight like Christ did, righteously, and Spirit-led. It is when we offer ourselves up to God, as a living sacrifice, then following His leading on a daily basis.

The Fight That Comes to You

Life is such that some fights are not at all that hard to find, because they come to you. Either through an observation, or an unraveling, or a real time event, your fight is staring you in the face. The only question in these moments is what kind of response you will give. Today, most people are of the mentality that if it doesn't involve me personally, it is not my fight. But that thinking is not what we are taught by Christ. Jesus engaged evil, albeit wisely, wherever He found it.

Whether it was men stoning a woman for adultery, or the money changers selling their wares at the synagogue, He was the

Man for the moment. And His actions always brought those acting wrongly to justice, saving those who would be victims.

The Risk of the Unseen

The unseen or the unknown is always going to be a problem to us. Especially when it comes to warfare. Because in war, we don't know what may be around the next corner. It takes courage to engage in an act when there is great potential of risk. However, a man cannot feel completely alive without embracing risk.

Many of us spend our energy and creativity trying to eliminate risk, or attempting to squeeze it down to a more manageable size. But risk that is manageable does not need faith. If a man succeeds in securing his life against all risk, he regresses into a cocoon of self-protection and then wonders why he feels he is suffocating.

One Sunday early in my life began like most. My brothers, sister, and I were rousted out of bed by dad to get ready for church. I think I was about 14 at the time and everything went smoothly as we boarded our old Pontiac and exited the driveway toward Saint Mary's Catholic church for Sunday mass. During the drive, something drew my attention to what was happening in front of a house along our path. A man had a woman on the ground in front of a house, and he was beating her. When I alerted my dad, he looked over and saw the same scene.

His immediate reaction was to calmly turn the car around and go to the aid of this woman. Our car came to a stop in front of the house and my dad exited the car and told the man, in no uncertain terms, to stop what he was doing. The abuser screamed profanities at my dad and told him it was none of his business, because it was his wife. Then he picked her up and threw her onto the porch of the house, apparently attempting to get her inside.

Before he could do it, my father calmly walked to the man, picked him up, and carried him out to the grass, dropping him there. He stood over the man and told him not to get up several times. While he was telling a watching neighbor to call the police, the man stood up and cocked his arm back intending to punch my father. In what seemed like a flash, that abusive man was out cold on the ground. When the police arrived, instead of arresting dad, the police thanked him.

Then they told my father how often they were called out to this house to deal with the same situation. And they made it clear that he deserved what my father gave him. When it was over, my father walked to the car and we continued to church. We were late but we made it to mass, and nothing more was said by my father about the incident. My father did not have it in him to turn away from injustice. He was a man of action when there was an opportunity to help those who could not help themselves.

While my father was not necessarily acting at the leading of the Holy Spirit, I cannot help but think it was the right thing to do. He could have just kept driving and forgot about it, which is what most would have done. But that day his actions resulted in the saving of a victim and the incarceration of a tyrant. That fight didn't come to my dad because of anything he did. He didn't provoke it, ask for it, or do anything toward the abusive man.

Conversely, many fights come to us that we would never ask for. They can come through natural disasters like the earthquakes in Nepal, or an act of war like the bombing of Pearl Harbor, or through an attack like the one on the Twin Towers in New York. They can come through a disease, loss, and economic or social turmoil. Life is such that these are not all that uncommon. The problem is, as we become more and more "modern," we become less and less adept at springing to action to fight in these kinds of situations. Our faith requires us to be ready. Our readiness as warriors is our responsibility and needs to cover the entire spectrum of our existence: body, soul, and spirit.

In my travels, I have found myself in many fights I wasn't looking for, doing things I didn't think I could do. Whether it was in a bunker across the Gaza Strip, in the Himalayas flying in a small helicopter over death and destruction, or in the most Islamic nation in the world, fights found me. But to those who are led by the Holy Spirit, the faith needed to face any fight regardless of how it presents itself is available. God obviously placed me there because He trusted me to believe in His divine deliverance.

The Fight to Defend the Church

An entire book could be written about the defense of the faith: what it is, what it is not. Historically, it isn't too difficult to see that the idea of defending our faith has been done wrong more than it has been done right. So, I will make this easy for you. Here are appropriate measures:

1.   **Arm yourself with correct apologetic.**

The apostle Peter said in I Peter 3:15 (NKJV), "Always be ready to give a defense to everyone who asks you a reason for the hope that is in you."

I am the type of person who loves a good debate. In fact, when someone is attacking the veracity of Scripture or anything along those lines, I am in my element. I have learned not to become emotional in a debate; rather, I simply respond to the specifics of the circumstances. Whether it is with a knock at my door, or a heckling in a crowd, I love it. One of the reasons I enjoy this is because I have taken the time to educate myself so I have answers when asked. I pay attention to the world I live in, because it is the battlefield.

The Bible is an easy target because it is a book given down by God to men, written by men, and much of its contents are only accepted by faith. But in thousands of years, nothing has even come close to beating it. The principles within it work and its wisdom is unmatched. We must not only read the Bible to know it, but to know it so well that we can defend it. We must recognize a counterfeit on sight no matter how holy it seems. And we must know Jesus so well that no matter how many come saying they are Jesus, we instinctively know the truth.

In the days preceding the coming of Christ, we are told that a great deceit will fall upon mankind. Many false Christs will come, with signs and wonders, seeking to deceive even the leaders of the church. We defend the church by knowing our enemy, studying his tactics, and preparing ourselves.

2.   Protect the church against itself.

An argument can be made that more destructive things have been done by the church against itself than by those who don't even believe. When Christians enter into strife it is like opening the door to all the devils of hell. Few things grieve the Lord more than when His people, for whom He died, refuse to deal with their issues, causing strife in the body. Arguments can break out virtually on every level. So, how do I fight it? By remembering who the Head of that church is, and following His word.

3.   Be willing to go into all of the world.

Jesus told His disciples, "Go into all the world and preach the gospel to all creation." This was not just given to the twelve disciples. It applies to anyone who believes in Christ. The world is a big place. And what about "all creation?" Many see this as too big and for the most part give up. It is a fight to obey such an admonition.

But Christ placed you where you are. Your fight to bring Christ to others begins by allowing Him to use your life in the world He has placed you. That is where it begins and as long as you make yourself available, He will lead you from there. As Isaiah 41:10 (NKJV) reads, "Fear not, for I *am* with you; Be not dismayed, for I *am* your God. I will strengthen you, Yes, I will help you, I will uphold you with My righteous right hand."

CHAPTER 13

THE MISSION

My entire adult life I have been infatuated with the notion that men can actually hear the voice of God. To me, it is clear that God is speaking, and I am not simply referring to the process of reading Scripture. Yeah, yeah, I know that the written word is the judge of all that is spoken, but in my Christian experience that which has truly had meaning came as a direct result of the Bible speaking and me hearing.

I mean really hearing! Or should I say processing? I guess it is all the same to me. As finite beings we filter most of life through our senses. But we know that the God-touched spirit man is not limited to those senses. That spirit man is able to see things and hear things and process life through other than rational means. It is kind of scary isn't it? The thought that most people live out their entire lives having never heard? Having never connected with the trans-rational, which is holy, without any flaw, and wise beyond all human understanding?

I'm aware of all the excuses we make as so-called legit reasons why we cannot or should not connect with heaven this way. No need to enumerate, I have uttered most of them myself. What is interesting to me though is that in all my weakness and with all the messes I have gotten into because I did not make that connection, God still makes it all come out right in the end, as long as I made the change and tuned in. It is clear to me that God is even able to correct a life's worth of messes with just one connection.

We have been taught to listen to others talk about Scripture, and mostly leave it at that. It is not that there is anything really wrong with this. God set among us men and women whose calling is to speak to us about Scripture. They deserve honor and have been, up to this point, the primary speakers of God's will to us. So, looking back, how has that worked out for you?

As believers, we still have bucket-loads of problems. Most of us just come to the place where we choose to live with it. We conclude that all our dysfunction is never going to change and we go to church and Bible studies filtering everything that is said through that dysfunction, which is a sure way to assure that we don't grow in our relationship with God.

The world is changing! The question is, are we? The change in our world is progressively moving toward more and more evil. Shouldn't we as Christians be matching or surpassing that evil with the greater power of connection? Listen, it is impossible to connect with God and not have it change you. So, the obvious question is, are you changing? If not, then the only reason is a lack of connection, and I am talking about more than sermons.

Truth is, sermons don't set us free unless they are met with a hearer who knows how to process it. It is not the speaker's responsibility to bring change to the hearer. It is up to the hearer to take what is spoken to a higher level of processing for that truth to be life altering. Truth sets men free, or should I say that it is the truth we own that sets us free.

God didn't put a moratorium on truth to be delivered Sundays only or through any particular person or clergy. We were not given people to speak God's word to us with the process ending there. God's Word is alive and the agent of life. It is the single most powerful gift Christ gave the church.

But to have a life-changing effect on those who hear it, engagement must happen! The process of change God intended for every Christian can only happen through engagement. That engagement always begins with a question. Then it can go to a wrestling match with God. Or it can go to a relentless prayer or petition. Or it can go to a challenge to others in fellowship.

I cannot believe that we serve a God who has chosen not to be available. Isn't that the whole reason Jesus came to this miserable piece of dirt, to redeem and to restore? Most Christians have the redemption thing down, but what about the restore part? What was the first "natural" thing that happened when Jesus died on the cross? In the eyes of all men the curtain that separated all men up to that time from personal interaction with God ripped in half. You think God was attempting to get something across to us about His priority through this act? Obviously, the answer is yes!

He wanted to connect with all His people again. It hadn't happened since the garden of Eden. But because of Christ's sacrifice on the cross every man and woman would be allowed to go to God directly, no hindrances, no stop signs, just the words, "Come to me." Jesus came to restore fellowship and unhindered connection with the godhead.

Is it enough that we know that we are saved? I say no! I want more, because the Father sent His only Son to provide me with unlimited access to God and all of His gifts. I am not satisfied and you shouldn't be either. Scripture is intended to be God's initiator of dramatic change. When we read it, we become hungry and thirsty. We want more. Then we begin to ask for it. More Lord, I want more! That cry is one the Holy Spirit always responds to. Always. Remember, faith comes by hearing and hearing by the Word of God. We must make a habit of reading Scripture in such a manner where we are left inquiring of God: "Lord, take me deeper, let me see what is not obvious."

Seeing More

Maybe it is time to exercise this process. I will start by using a commonly known passage from Jeremiah 29:11. There has been a great deal taught about this passage and some good books have been written about it. As I look over the teachings, it seems to me that the main, life-changing part of the passage has possibly been missed. Scripture is supposed to edify us while at the same time challenge us.

Often, we love the edify part but many of us don't catch the challenge. Because if we were brutally honest with ourselves we would have to admit that most of us do not want to be challenged! We want life to be "normal." No surprises, no more than what we deem enough.

"For I know the thoughts that I think toward you, says the Lord, thoughts of peace and not of evil, to give you a future and a hope." Question? Is it enough simply to know that God is thinking "good thoughts?"

Is a good thought really good if I am not aware what that good thought is? Even though I know that the thought is one of peace and not evil, I want to know more. Isn't that the way the Lord made us? To explore is what makes life fun. And I want to have fun as a follower of Christ.

If I told my wife that I was thinking good thoughts about her, she would be happy for about five seconds. Then she would want to know what those good thoughts were. She is not really edified by the simple knowledge of knowing that I am thinking good thoughts, she wants specific details: Is it about a trip or a vacation? Is it that I am pretty to you? Is it that you are going to surprise me with something?

And what does it mean when the Lord says He is thinking thoughts "toward me?" Why not, about me? It is strategic that God used the word toward because it carried with it the connotation of movement or sending. For instance, I am driving *toward* home, or a package is on its way *toward* you.

Lastly, what does it mean when God says, "to give us an expected end?" What is this "expected end?" If it is expected, then there has to be a predetermined outcome. So, I must conclude that God has a predetermined end for me. But that end is not attainable unless I know in detail the directions. Can I get to the expected end that God has in mind for me without knowing more details?

And yet most people I meet who know this passage have never asked for specifics regarding the direction for their life. Most simply accept the ethereal idea that God is in control and He will lead me. That is how we justify our lack of engagement with God. Rather then pressing God for specifics, we accept religious platitudes and the distant relationship that will surely be the outcome. God's "good thoughts" are supposed to be known to me. He is sending them toward me, to my spirit, so that through those specific thoughts I will end my life having reached my specific life's purpose. Asking God for specifics is essential to success in the Christian experience.

CHAPTER 14

BOOTS ON THE GROUND

The goal of the Christian faith is occupation. Jesus said, "Go into all the world and preach the gospel." When that is done right, the result is conversion of both people and societies. This is occupation, and lest we think this statement is a little militant, let me remind you of something. Our message is THE only message resulting in true freedom for man. Every other message not founded upon the truth of holy Scripture is a lie and results in eternal hell for those deceived by it.

This fact gives new meaning to the mission field. In the past, we have always known the mission field as a place most people really don't want to go. But we are more than willing to throw money at those who are. We expect them to learn the language, love the people, and spend their lives preaching the gospel to poor lost ones. There is only one thing wrong with this idea. When we send men and women onto a mission field, we are sending them to war. Not only are they going to a land where people believe a lie, but the people are controlled by the enemies of our faith.

It was a Saturday and I was multitasking life as usual. I was working on this manuscript and when I needed a break, I would mow the lawn. Then I heard an unfamiliar sound: our doorbell.

Almost no one who comes to our house rings the doorbell. It is understood around our home to just walk in and announce yourself or be shot. As I walked though our large foyer I noticed two women standing at the door smiling widely. While I was hoping they were from the Publishers Clearing House to announce I had won millions, reality hit when I greeted them.

"Hello sir, we would like to invite you to a world changing event," one said as she handed me a pamphlet. The older woman began to speak but I interrupted. I asked them if they were Jehovah's Witnesses. She said, "Yes we are." She attempted to continue but again, in a respectful way, I interrupted her. I said that I was all too familiar with the teachings of the Watchtower and their distortion of holy Scripture to fit their heretical lies. I made it clear that while I was not attacking them, the organization they represented was leading people to hell and encouraged them to reconsider their commitment.

The older woman spoke up at that point. She said, "Well sir, I used to be a Baptist but realized about ten years ago that being a Jehovah's Witness was the true way." At that point I felt nothing but holy anger because standing in front of me was a poor soul who Satan had stolen from the true faith. Baptists believe in the major tenets of the Christian faith and as such are believers. I was not going to let her leave my porch without knowing what a great mistake she had made. She had not just changed churches; she abandoned Jesus Christ and the Christian faith when she became a Jehovah's Witness.

So I said to her, "Ma'am, I respect your right to believe what you want. But I am not sure anyone has told you of the consequences of your decision." I continued, "Ma'am, based upon what you have told me, the Bible declares you an apostate, because you have denied the true faith, exchanging the truth for a lie. You would have been better off having never knowing Christ than to have come to know Him and then reject your faith."

Once I finished, I remained silent, waiting for a reply. But there was no comeback. As they thanked me for my time and turned to leave, I offered to pray for them to recommit to Christ but they just walked off. After closing the door, I asked the Lord to cause those words to echo in their ears, giving them no rest until they surrendered once again to Christ.

One of the problems with Christianity today is our lack of frankness. A dying person doesn't need platitudes, nice sayings, or political correctness. They need life support. When someone is going to hell, they need to know it. But how we communicate that is of the utmost importance. The methods of misguided groups like Westboro Baptist are useless because they misrepresent our God and do nothing but create ill will for the kingdom of God.

Conversely, when God opens a door, either to speak the truth to someone personally or to a crowd, there should be no question when all is said and done, that without Christ, hell awaits. Of course, with that revealed, we need to give those lost a glimpse of heaven, letting them know that love unspeakable is awaiting them from the One who gave all to save them. This interchange is spiritual warfare at it's best. Heaven against hell, life against death, truth against lies. To communicate this is no different than combat in war.

"Boots on the Ground" is part of a message we have been speaking around the world where people are struggling with war, famine, persecution, and unrest. It is a message that reminds them of the promise God gave Joshua and Moses in Joshua 1:3…"I will give you every place where you set your foot, as I promised Moses."

The concept of boots on the ground is also a military term that underscores the idea of taking possession of the battlefield. When a soldier places his boots on the ground it is for one purpose, to take the ground. When life comes apart it is easy to just capitulate. But we have learned through the example of the heroes of faith, that if we trust God in these times and commit to fight, God will meet us there, and give us the victory. It all starts with the commitment of "boots on the ground."

Nehemiah's Challenge

The story of Nehemiah is amazing. It is a classic example of a man who heard God's call and committed himself to restoration of something God loved: Jerusalem. In the twentieth year of Artaxerxes, king of Persia, Nehemiah was cupbearer to the king. Upon learning that the remnant in Judah were in distress and that the walls of Jerusalem were broken down, he asked the king for permission to return and rebuild the city. Nehemiah was an important man. As the cupbearer of the king, his job status was at the top. In short, he had it made.

Often as believers, the Holy Spirit interrupts our daily life. And when this happens, we begin to care about things we never thought we would concern ourselves with. When we accept the task associated with this interruption, what we had previously deemed important changes dramatically. In Nehemiah's case, he was willing to place his posh position and job on the line because of what God was calling him to do.

When Jesus is Lord of your life, He alone has the right to change your direction. And while this may cause us some discomfort due to the change, the fact that God trusts us with His will, is the greatest of all honors for us. Nehemiah took the position in life to make a difference. For him, it was not enough just to have a great career and enjoy his life. He lived to make a difference. When he was made aware that the city of God, Jerusalem, was in shambles, he laid everything down and decided to change things.

Artaxerxes sent him to Judah as governor of the province with a mission to rebuild, letters explaining his support for the venture, and provision for timber from the king's forest. Once there, Nehemiah defied the opposition of Judah's enemies on all sides—Samaritans, Ammonites, Arabs, and Philistines—and rebuilt the walls within 52 days!

Today it is typical for people to talk about what is wrong with the world. But all too often that is all it is, talk. God is looking for men who are more action than talk. There is nothing more powerful than a man who lets his actions do the talking for him, especially if those actions result in personal attack or deep personal sacrifice. When we understand that resistance is unavoidable when we follow God, a peace comes. And with that peace come resolve and courage.

Nehemiah was a man on fire. Once he decided to move, he would not be stopped. You see, there were people who not only were responsible for the destruction of Jerusalem, but they were bent on keeping it that way. They were happy with something grievous to God. So when a man showed up to deal with it they chose to fight him, thinking he would quickly retreat. But that would not happen.

Nehemiah had to make changes to his plan because of the resistance, but he took it in stride, continuing the mission to restore. Real men on a real mission do not have a plan for defeat. The opposite is true. What Nehemiah shows us is that if we stay focused, God will meet us there, giving us the power and wisdom to succeed.

One of the great things I have learned over 30 years of serving God is how great His favor is. Literally, every time I have launched out to follow His leading, He met my move with favor and provision that has no natural explanation. And that is His promise. If we move in faith, He moves to make our path full of miracles. Nehemiah began his journey to follow God's leading in prayer.

As Nehemiah 1:4-5 reads, "So it was, when I heard these words, that I sat down and wept, and mourned for *many* days; I was fasting and praying before the God of heaven. And I said: 'I pray, Lord God of heaven, O great and awesome God....'" Preparation of our heart for God's mission cannot be overemphasized. We cannot just fake this. Nehemiah knew that his success was dependent upon the spirit of a man being fully led by the Holy Spirit.

Having said that, after Nehemiah prayed, he departed to do God's will. And he didn't tell anyone about his mission. Upon arriving, people began showing up and presenting themselves as servants to him and his mission. When we are available to God, He makes sure others who are also available are drawn together with us like a magnet.

It is interesting to me that so many of God's people just accepted the deplorable conditions of Jerusalem for so long before Nehemiah decided to do something about it. And there is something we can take away from this. Sometimes, because we are so used to our surroundings, we don't notice those things that grieve God. It takes someone who is not familiar with our world to bring our attention to it.

Apparently, God couldn't find a man in Jerusalem to deal with the situation. So he looked and found a man in Nehemiah. And the moment Nehemiah arrived on the scene, others' blinders fell off, and they came to him to offer their help. Think about this today. In your surroundings, what may be deplorable to God that you don't even notice anymore? Ask God to cause your blinders to fall off.

There are times when God leads us to do something great that others don't think much about. This was the case with Nehemiah. He dedicated everything to the task of rebuilding the walls of Jerusalem. It has to be a surprise to Nehemiah when he learned of the opposition to his massive undertaking. And this opposition was not simply in words. This opposition involved weapons and a verbal commitment to undo all he was building.

His response was not to get depressed, slow down, or sow fear in his builders. His response was to tell every man building to work with one hand, and carry a sword with the other. I love this because it sets an example for us to follow when we are doing everything right, and opposition raises its ugly head. The message? Don't ignore opposition. Don't fear opposition. Keep doing what God has called you to do, intimidate the enemy with strength, and finish your task.

Nehemiah 6:15-16 reads, "So the wall was finished on the twenty-fifth day of Elul, in fifty-two days. And it happened, when all our enemies heard of it, and all the nations around us saw these things, that they were very disheartened in their own eyes; for they perceived that this work was done by our God." Many times, when we are in the midst of doing something God has led us to do, we are overcome by doubt. And we wonder if this was just a bad idea from the beginning. Brothers, this is normal. All the resistance and the unplanned events at times tend to lead us to this doubt. It is in these moments that we need the Holy Spirit to encourage us with the faith to reach the goal.

It is hard to believe that Nehemiah completed the work God called him to in just 52 days. He took on an impossible task, faced all his enemies, and completed the task. But that is not the most important thing to take away from this passage. What is amazing is, when Nehemiah refused to quit, everyone who resisted him realized that it was God who actually did the work. And this is the prime goal of all Christians: to bring glory to God through our actions. When I get to heaven I want to be able to give something to Jesus. I don't just want to transition into eternity having done nothing worthy of a crown. Any crowns of honor I receive in life are my gifts to Him in glory.

Finding Honor

The meaning of honor is "high moral standard of behavior." When Jesus accepted a will other than his own, He entered into the realm of honor. That is why we give Him all praise, honor, and glory. It is because His sacrifice earned Him all that and much more.

Years ago, I was privileged to attend the graduation of the Air Force special operations, "PJ's," or para-jumpers. These men are responsible for providing emergency and lifesaving services to our troops when they are wounded in combat. I was there with a friend and former PJ to attend his reunion and the graduation of a new class.

As we walked the corridors, the walls were filled with plaques and pictures of men who had served with distinction over the years. The awards included the Medal of Honor. Their motto is "That Others May Live: AF PJ's." Like many military mottos, I felt this one was a great one for my life as a believer. The reason I live, is so others can. This is the only way we can achieve honor: through sacrifice and putting others' welfare above our own. Honor is in short supply because we allow it to be. It is our legacy to walk in honor in this world.

It was a typical sunny spring San Diego Sunday morning and I awoke just in time to see the sunrise. Like always, I spent time in prayer and prepared for Sunday services. As I arrived at church my staff notified me that two "special operators" were being deployed overseas and would need prayer before they departed. This practice had become commonplace in the church because it consisted mostly of military men and women and their families.

Every week while I was home, I looked into the eyes of those who were waiting and believing that their loved ones would come home safe. Moms and children struggled through the months, counting the days until they could stop fighting worry and see their loved ones. I hate to say it but that look of worry and concern became so common to me that it didn't dig at me like it used to. I realized that after a brief encounter with a five-year-old boy named Jake while in the parking lot of our church that Sunday morning.

I was about to walk into our sanctuary when I noticed a mother trying to get her children out of the car. Her husband deployed the previous week to Iraq and she was dealing with all that was involved in deployment, now for the eighth time. I walked over to her car to help and was met by "the man of the house," the SEAL's five-year-old son. I picked him up to say hello and he instantly began to tell me a story. He said, "My daddy left us to go to Iraq. He will be gone for about seven months. I am the man of the house until he comes home."

His lips quivered as he spoke and it struck me that in the last two years he had seen his daddy, a navy SEAL chief, home for only about six months. I don't think it is a stretch to say that his father has only been home for about half his life. I just stood there holding him for a few more minutes, feeling like he was about to cry. But he held tough, like his mother who was holding his baby sister. They have no choice but to learn to tough it out. That's life as a military wife and child. They have no choice but to be tough. That's part of the deal, to tough it out.

That experience underscores what sacrifice really is about. Sometimes I wonder if we really know what it is to sacrifice here in America. It strikes me that so many of us live our lives not giving a moment's thought to anyone but ourselves. That is the reason honor is in such short supply.

In this final chapter, my hope is that you will make a commitment to live an honorable life. That you will look beyond self, knowing that Jesus Christ is reaching out to you, searching for a man or woman who will give Him a life He can defeat evil through, liberating the lost. To accept the call to warfare is to assure a good death. My friends, there's no other way to live.

This life is fleeting and compared to eternity is a flash. It doesn't matter where you're at right now, what defines you, or who people call you. You were made for greatness. What is God calling you to that goes beyond anything you're doing right now? You are a warrior. Called by God to fight. To sacrifice who you are so that others may live. That is a life of honor and God cannot wait to give you that distinction.

A *good* death is really a *godly* death. To know that we laid it all on the battlefield of life at that moment when we leave this world is the ultimate gift we give to ourselves and to the generations to come. As 1 Corinthians 15:55 reads, "Where, O death, is your victory? Where, O death, is your sting?"

There is no better place for me to end this book than with the words of the apostle Paul written to his spiritual son Timothy. The following was not intended to give Timothy a sendoff with a soft pat on the head, telling him to be good and live long. It was written by a man who would soon know a good death.

Scarred and bloodied in a life lived abandoned to God, Paul wanted his son to take it to the next level himself. He wanted him to stay in the fight, trusting in Jesus to carry him through every challenge to his faith into victory. His single desire was for Timothy to live life in such a way that he also would see a good death.

Paul wrote in Ephesians 6:10-12, "Finally, be strong in the Lord and in his mighty power. Put on the full armor of God so that you can take your stand against the devil's schemes. For our struggle is not against flesh and blood, but against the rulers, against the authorities, against the powers of this dark world and against the spiritual forces of evil in the heavenly realms."

Mortality is assured to all men, and while we may not be able to determine the time or the place we will die, we can be assured that however it comes, it will be a good death by fighting the good fight of faith until our last breath. Death is just the beginning of eternity for us, as all questions are answered, all restrictions on our earthly bodies are removed, and Jesus is seen as our wounded, yet victorious, warrior King. That is a good death!

PRAYER FOR WARRIORS

May God give you the courage to live your life to its fullest. And may He give you strength and wisdom to fight the good fight of faith so you finish well by walking in His ordained steps for your life until the day you see Him face to face. Amen!

ACKNOWLEDGMENTS

The process of writing this book took about two years. But the stories within came over decades. It is impossible to quantify the value of those I'm about to thank. But I will try.

Almost forty years ago I met Amber, the love of my life. Every day since she has walked this battlefield alongside me as a voice, friend, counselor, and lover. She was the first to read this manuscript. When I handed it to her I knew I was about to hear the brutal truth regarding its worth or lack thereof. As she read it over several days, I sneaked a peek many times wondering about the meaning of the look on her face. It was grueling. She has earned the right to judge me and is the one I trust most to tell it like it is. Then one day she asked to speak to me about the book. We sat down and then she smiled and continued to tell me what *A Good Death* meant to her. That day, a weight was lifted off my shoulders, and in its place, came boldness and faith. She is, and will always remain, my love, God's gift to me.

In the writing if this book I cannot overstate the value and input of my friend and fellow warrior, Kim Clement. Kim was the toughest man I have ever known. He gave everything in service to the Kingdom of God and there is no greater example of one who found a good death than Kim. His example of absolute focus, along with his dogged determination, set a high bar for others to follow. His wisdom compels me every day to press for more of God and to give my life for something worth dying for.

I also owe a debt to Every Nation and most specifically, its president, Steve Murrell. Steve is a stoic and determined leader with wisdom way beyond his years. His zeal for this book was second only to my wife Amber's as an encouragement to move forward.

Lastly, I want to thank one of my dearest friends, a former Navy SEAL, Jeff Bramstedt. Jeff embodies many of the principles written about in this book. A hero to this nation, a hero to those he mentors, and a treasure to the Kingdom of God, Jeff will carry the people of God into righteous battle long after I am gone. Strength and Honor, brother.

ENDORSEMENTS

It doesn't take a huge brain to come to the conclusion that as a culture we are quickly approaching demise from within our own borders. To add to that, we have adopted the instant gratification mindset, interest in our own comfort is paramount, and moral compasses have spun out of control. The availability of drugs, porn, sex, and things that are simple distractions, has made navigating the early stages of life most difficult for our children. What has been considered "right" is now "wrong", and what was once considered wrong, is not only acceptable, but has been established as a benchmark. In short, we have become a "society of the soft". This is a perfect breeding ground for enemy spiritual activity. Bottom line, we are under attack. These issues and many more are prevalent even to those who believe that Jesus came to earth, put on people gear, walked our streets, brought hope, and died for all of our sake, defeating this enemy and making His mark on this world and its inhabitants for all time. We must as believers, grasp these facts, take a stand against this defeated enemy who is still going to fight us, regardless of our battle-ground stance and presence, or lack thereof. Be the warrior that answers the call to engage. "A Good Death" will be the push to get you out of neutral.

Jeff Bramstedt
Former US Navy SEAL, CEO, Skydive San Diego
Director, Life of Valor Men's Conferences

There are some books you pick up and flip through, but this isn't one of them. Greg pulls you into his world from the first chapter and then opens up a world for you that you've never seen before. This book is captivating, illuminating, and authentic. This is one of those rare books that takes you on a journey into territory you thought you knew only to discover the subject has aspects you've never seen. Read it and see for yourself!

Dr. Lance Wallnau
Lance Learning Group

Inside every man is the heart of a warrior. From childhood, it's as if an innate desire to be strong, fight, and win pushes us to pursue the understanding of what it means to truly be a man. With that pursuit also comes a desired validation that we are becoming or have become the man that our families, our friends, our God, and we ourselves would be proud of. But the sad truth that is ever present in today's society is that there are few men actually modeling and teaching what it means to be a man after God's own heart. As a result, many are left to figure it out for themselves while observing the facades projected by the media and other men they may admire that are posing and making their own assumptions about manhood in blind pursuits (and quite honestly, failing miserably at it). The truth is that there is a real enemy influencing men...and he's often winning.

Subsequently (and I believe ignorantly), the church has produced an authoritatively emasculated generation of men who expect a "participation trophy," a pat on the back, and for God to fix whatever is broken for them, instead of the warriors who know their God, seize their authority, take the battle to their enemy, and realize that if they don't fight then their relationships, families, ministries, and very lives may hang in the balance.

In writing *A Good Death*, Greg Wark has ignited the heart of the warrior and with a father's wisdom has presented a path of understanding about how to think, respond, and fight to leave it all on the battlefield at the end of our lives as the men that God has called all of us to be!

Aaron D. Davis
Retired S.W.A.T./Detective Sergeant

At a recent minister's conference, a sobering statistic was presented: more than 50 percent of present day pastors were launched into ministry during or shortly after the Jesus People movement and Charismatic renewal of the 1970s and early 1980s. This tells us that the church is in a time of great transition, a trepidatious time in terms of leadership in the church. Many of the 50 percent, now in their sixties and seventies, are holding on to leadership for all it is worth, rather than nurturing and preparing the next generation to go farther than we have as leaders. Further, and quite sadly, many of the present leadership are not finishing well. Rather than stepping into fathering roles for the next generation, they are leaving the work of God disgruntled, wounded, and broken. It does not have to be that way.

In this thoughtful and compassionate work by my friend, Dr. Greg Wark, principles necessary to finish strong and fulfill one's destiny of a good death are presented with powerful illustrations that speak to the heart of the matter. This is not a book for the leader in denial or the parishioner looking for something simple and sweet to eat. It will take guts to get the glory God intends us to experience, and much of what is needed to finish as men and women of God, strong as Jesus, you will find in this book.

Stan E. DeKoven, Ph.D., MFT
President, Vision International University

18239809R00120

Printed in Poland
by Amazon Fulfillment
Poland Sp. z o.o., Wrocław